Freedom, Resp␣␣ the M␣

To Jackie

best wishes

Gary

Gary Taylor

With a Foreword by Donald Trelford

Sheffield Hallam University Press
Learning Centre
City Campus
Sheffield S1 1WB

Cover designed and typeset by Design Studio, Learning Centre, Sheffield Hallam University

Printed by Print Unit, Sheffield Hallam University

©2000 ISBN 0 86339 874 X

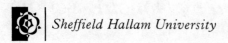 *Sheffield Hallam University*

Contents

Acknowledgements

I would like to thank those who helped in the publication of this book. My thanks go to Vaughan Taylor for designing the cover, Karen Guymer for help with proof reading, and Monica Moseley at SHU for publishing the final result. My thanks also to Donald Trelford for his thoughtful foreword, and to my students for their willingness to debate.

Foreword

Most journalists, in my experience, start out on their career with what David Astor, the former *Observer* editor, called "a strong whiff of idealism". This can take different forms, some of them overtly or covertly political, but the one common characteristic is a desire, even a compulsion, to tell the truth about the world they live in, combined with a readiness to challenge official versions of that reality. This picture of youthful idealists setting themselves against authority may seem strange to those who regard the media as a crudely commercial operation engaged in boosting private profit by trivial, sensational and unscrupulous means. It is certainly at odds with the public perception of journalists as cynical hacks who would sell their own grandmother in pursuit of a good story. The interplay between the forces of idealism and the forces of cynicism for possession of a journalist's soul goes to the heart of the debate about the modern media.

That is why a book like this, examining the vaunted claims of the media against the market-place realities, is a useful aid to public understanding. Words like "freedom" and "responsibility" can mean all things to all men. I was once in a public debate with Tony Benn when he argued for "the freedom to be *irr*esponsible". By this he meant that a prime requirement, almost a definition of a free press is that no body should determine where the line between "responsible" and "irresponsible" journalism should be drawn. The problem with this argument is that the very power of the press to influence politics and to shape people's lives and attitudes is such that society feels entitled to some degree of control, if only to protect itself against what it regards as the media's excesses. How to exercise that control without infringing the citizen's democratic right to freedom of expression (and its corollary, the freedom to hear that expression) is still an unresolved issue in Britain at the end of the twentieth century.

I remember an editor saying, in reply to a difficult question: "There are some questions in this life to which we know the answer. There are some questions to which there may be an answer, but we don't happen to know what it is. There are some questions, however, to which there are *no* answers - and I fear your question falls into that category." The question implicit in much of the political debate about the media – "What is the right balance between freedom and responsibility?" – also falls into that unanswerable category.

So what do we do? In the end we may have to make an unpalatable choice. Do we prefer to live in a society in which filth and lies are published or one in which the content of the media is controlled? To my mind, while the first choice is undesirable, the latter is unthinkable in any society that dares to call itself free. Working between those extremes are those who draft and apply codes of conduct for self-regulation. These people tend to be abused on both sides – by the public for failing to curb excesses of pornography or intrusions into privacy; by the media for threatening their freedom to publish what they want. But theirs may be the only way of squaring this circular moral dilemma.

How, then, can the media have reached this low point in public esteem if journalists are idealists at heart? The answer is that newspapers and broadcasting organisations are not owned by journalists or run for their benefit. The work done by journalists fills only a part of a complex commercial jigsaw in which advertising and circulation revenue constitute the bottom line. I once had a general manager who said: "For me, journalists are simply a non-profit-making department, like drivers or security men". Rupert Murdoch is said to have described the role of journalists in the digital age as that of "bit providers". The more successful and enterprising media organisations, however, are generally those that hold their journalists in higher regard, recognising the commercial truth of Lord Thomson's remark that "editorial holds the key to everything else". The only time I met that legendary figure, who once owned *The Times* and the *Sunday Times* as part of a global media empire, was when he sent me off to edit one of his African papers with the inspirational message ringing in my ears: "You make a dollar for me, boy, and I'll make a dollar for you!"

While in Africa I experienced my first serious pressure as an editor, when a politician threatened to destroy Lord Thomson's presses unless I gave him more favourable publicity. In general, however, the pressures on journalists to temper what they write in the interests of something other than the whole truth come in more subtle disguises. Advertising is one such force, but in my experience this pressure is rarely applied crudely. I have come across no cases, for example, certainly not on a paper like *The Observer*, of a journalist being required to change some negative comments for fear of offending an advertiser. But there are certainly some parts of newspapers, usually in the consumer areas like travel, motoring and property, where the choice of subject and the editorial treatment dance to a tune set by the advertisement department.

In a period of 32 years I worked for several kinds of owner, from a charitable trust to multinational companies. While I was Editor, I saw it as my function to protect my journalists from any sense that the owner was peeping over their shoulder as they typed, or that they should take account of the owner's special interests in what they wrote. In this I was mostly, but not entirely, successful, for one owner, the Lonrho conglomerate led by the late "Tiny" Rowland, involved *The Observer*'s business pages in the company's battle with Mohammed Fayed over the ownership of the Harrods stores group. I believe that the integrity of the newspaper's coverage of this matter was subsequently vindicated by a Department of Trade Inspectors' Report, which supported the main allegations we had made. Later revelations added further support. Nonetheless, the public perception, stimulated by rival newspapers, that *The Observer* had served the commercial interests of its proprietor was undoubtedly damaging to a publication whose main asset (in some ways its only one) had always been its reputation for plain dealing.

Business reporting is, in many cases, a dubious activity, in that some newspapers tend to support the companies prepared to speak to them and to criticise those who speak to their rivals. Increasingly, this process is orchestrated by City of London public relations firms who are the business equivalent of political "spin doctors". It is used particularly at the time of business mergers. If a journalist is thought to be "on our side", then they grant him or her privileged information denied to everyone else. Likewise, a critic will be starved of information or excluded from private briefings. The same sort of process can be seen in political reporting through the lobby system, except that political reporters can usually find alternative sources of information.

I have never experienced pressure from an owner to bend the newspaper's political line, though I was always ready to discuss the paper's politics with anyone, especially members of the company's board, who seemed to me to have every right to express an opinion as long as the final decision was left to me. *The Observer* was rare, however, in being genuinely independent of party affiliations and in having the editor's independence enshrined in the company's articles of association and guaranteed by specially appointed directors. The groups that own the *Telegraph* or the *Mail* newspapers, on the other hand, are firmly committed to the Conservative cause and an editor who changed that approach without consulting his owner could reasonably expect to be censured. Likewise, on the other side of the political divide, with the *Mirror* group. The group most often quoted as being subject to an owner's whims or changing political allegiances is News International, whose chairman is Rupert Murdoch. These newspapers have also been accused of promoting Murdoch's interests in satellite television and, on one celebrated occasion, of toning down criticism of Communist China because of his commercial investments in that country.

It has never seemed to me to be a problem for society that some newspapers take strong or even perverse political positions, as long as they do not distort the news to fit those positions – and, crucially, as

V

long as there is a diversity of newspapers expressing a range of opinions. Ideally, newspapers should permit varying opinions to be expressed on particular issues, either through columnists with contrasting views or through their correspondence columns. I detect an increased willingness among editors to publish pro-and-anti articles on contentious issues to allow the readers to make up their own minds. It used to be said that newspapers exist to inform, to instruct and to entertain. Of the three, the entertainment function is now uppermost, even among so-called quality papers, because of the intensity of competition in the market-place; the process described as "dumbing down". This is partly a response to the fact that information is increasingly available to readers through television, radio and the Internet before the newspaper is published, forcing the papers into a reactive role and seeking to widen their appeal through more popular features and photographs.

For all the bewildering changes in technology, the transaction between writer and reader or viewer remains essentially the same: making sense of a complicated world. For this reason, I believe newspapers will survive the digital revolution, because they process raw information in a form and context that make it intelligible, and they are also easy to carry around. Their commercial equations will change, however, as the Internet claims more of their advertising. The media have a vested interest in the survival of a democratic society, because that is the only political context in which they can survive; in no other kind of society has a free press been allowed. Whether their morals will improve in the future, or they will show more social responsibility, remains to be seen. The answer depends on that eternal battle for the journalist's soul.

DONALD TRELFORD has been Professor of Journalism Studies at Sheffield University since 1994. From 1975-93 he was Editor of The Observer, during which period it was twice named Newspaper of the Year. In 1984 Trelford himself was commended as International Editor of the Year "for advancing press freedom and fostering journalistic excellence". He is now President of the Media Society, a columnist for the Daily Telegraph and a member of the Newspaper Panel of the Competitions Commission.

1. Freedom and responsibility

Freedom has become one of the most treasured features of western democratic societies. During the height of the cold war, it was something that western leaders claimed that we had and the eastern bloc lacked. This freedom was said to include free elections, freedom of speech, freedom of lifestyle and a free media. A free media is reputed to be one free from government ownership and control, one that operates independently of any political faction, and monitors public life on our behalf. Such expectations, however, neglect to consider the vested interests of owners, the personal agendas of editors, the social perspectives of journalists, and the pressures brought to bear through competition for a share in the market. A free media does not necessarily serve the public interest or behave in a responsible manner.

Freedom of the media is often defended on the grounds that it contributes towards uncovering the truth, and that a free media can act as an effective check on the powers of government[1]. In the United States, for example, the constitutional guarantee of freedom of expression is meant to give the media 'breathing room' so that they can opt to act in a responsible manner. The American media have found that when they act irresponsibly, there has been an increase in public and government pressure to curtail the freedom of the media and increase their responsibilities. It is argued that '... both freedom and responsibility are important if the mass media are to function properly in society'[2]. Increasingly, those who monitor the media are pointing out that the free media should also assume some social responsibilities. The so-called social responsibility theory argues that the media have obligations to society. These obligations include providing information, allowing a diversity of views to be expressed,

[1] R. Negrine, *Politics and the Mass Media in Britain*, Routledge: London, 1994, p25.

[2] A.D. Gordon and J. Kittross, *Controversies in Media Ethics*, Longman: New York, 1999 (second edition), p26.

encouraging debate and nurturing good journalistic practice. It recognises that the media have to take on certain responsibilities or they will be imposed by outside bodies[3].

The relationship between freedom and responsibility can be approached in a variety of ways. A conceptual approach could take apart these terms, look at the variety of ways in which they are used, and attempt to identify any common features. An historical approach could look at the way that freedom and responsibility have been interpreted through history. It could show, for example, the way that responsibility was emphasised during the Middle Ages and freedom during the early modern period. It could also be approached ideologically. This would look at different ideological perspectives on the relationship between these two concepts. All of these approaches have their merits and can do a great deal to illuminate the relationship between freedom and responsibility. This study attempts to combine the ideological and the historical approaches. We begin by looking at the relationship between freedom and responsibility; in debates over the value of freedom of speech, in the fight for a free press in Britain, and in the way that the British media are regulated and constrained.

Free speech

The ideas of freedom and responsibility are central to debates over the true value of free speech. We might in the abstract claim that we have (or should have) the right to free speech. But does this mean that we should be able to exercise this right regardless of social consequences. Should the violent and the intolerant be afforded the same right to express their views as the virtuous ? When expressing our views, should we take into account the feelings, interests and safety of others or simply state the truth as we know it ?. In discussing these issues, theorists are often caught attempting to balance freedom and responsibility. Libertarians tend to emphasise freedom over all other considerations; this can be seen in many forms

---

[3] Negrine, *Politics and the Mass Media in Britain*, p25.

of liberalism. Those on the left and right, however, tend to view this freedom in the context of broader social responsibilities. This tension will be examined by looking at different ideological perspectives on freedom of speech, and using the Rushdie affair to illuminate some of the differences.

The classic liberal defence of freedom of speech was put forward by John Stuart Mill in his 1859 publication *On Liberty*. Mill argued that it was important to be tolerant of other opinions and to promote the right of free speech. He felt, in particular, that it was wrong for the government to silence diverse opinions. If the opinion was `right', it deprived the audience of the opportunity of exchanging error for truth. If the opinion was `wrong', we lose the opportunity to test our beliefs. Mill assumed that the truth will eventually prevail and that error can not withstand the power of truth. We therefore have nothing to fear from the expression of falsehoods[4].

Mill believed that suppressing opinions would be counter-productive. He points out that intellectual intolerance does not destroy opinions but `... induces men to disguise them, or to abstain from any active effort for their diffusion'[5]. In Mill's view, intolerance of diverse opinion cramps the intellectual development of the individual (by placing limits upon what can be thought), protects `heresies' from the scrutiny of free discussion, and degrades the intellectual atmosphere necessary for the growth of great thinkers[6]. Mill believes that it is impossible for us to know whether any opinions we try to suppress are false and that, even if we could be sure of this, it would still be an evil thing to do. Those who attempt to suppress opinions do so on the assumption that they are personally infallible. For Mill, we are all fallible. None of us has the right nor authority to decide what others should think and be allowed to express. He pointed out that those ideas that have dominated history have only done so for a limited time. The dominant opinions of each age change

---

[4] J.S. Mill, *On Liberty*, p20 in S. Collini (ed), *On Liberty and other writings*, Cambridge University Press: Cambridge, 1989, pp1-116.

[5] Mill, *On Liberty*, p34.

[6] Mill, *On Liberty*, pp35-36.

over time; thus illustrating that each age or epoch is fallible[7]. It would seem, therefore, that Mill is arguing that what we know as the truth changes over time. If we attempt to suppress opinions, we are preventing truth from developing. This would lead to intellectual and moral stagnation, for our species would be restrained from going beyond certain prescribed ideas.

Having access to a diverse range of opinions is, for Mill, beneficial to the truth. We can only assume that opinions are true if they have not been refuted . This means that there must be the opportunity to refute them. He claimed that the complete liberty of `... contradicting and disproving our opinion, is the very condition which justifies us in assuming its truth for purposes of action; and on no other terms can a being with human faculties have any rational assurance of being right'[8]. For the truth to prosper, we need to be able to combine our opinions with others. By dealing with the criticisms of our opinions, we increase our understanding and gain the right to think our `... judgement better than that of any person, or any multitude, who have not gone through a similar process'[9]. All doctrines, according to Mill, should be open to refutation. `Evil' opinions should not be suppressed for this can damage the truth. We should be able to defend the opinions we hold[10]. Mill's argument shows that a vibrant intellectual life requires constant scrutiny and movement. It does not rely upon learning a stock of truths, but in contributing (in whatever way we can) to new perspectives on life.

Mill moved on to argue that even if an opinion is known to be `true', discussion is still needed in order to avoid it becoming a dead dogma. Without discussion, our opinions become weak. We need to remember the roots of our opinions, and be able to defend them. If we only ever know one side of a case, we will be unable to argue against its opposite. Without discussion, the opinions we hold may become stale and lifeless. Mill warned against the `deep slumber of a

---

[7] Mill, *On Liberty*, pp20-22.
[8] Mill, *On Liberty*, p23.
[9] Mill, *On Liberty*, p24
[10] Mill, *On Liberty*, p25.

decided opinion' and claimed that the `... fatal tendency of mankind to leave off thinking about a thing when it is no longer doubtful, is the cause of half our errors'[11].

Mill was not hostile towards truths becoming established. Rather, he was an advocate of negative logic. This is where we point to the weaknesses in the truths we hold, not as an end in itself, but with the aim of strengthening our convictions. He thought that there should be some guidelines for discussion. It was important to avoid the suppression of facts and arguments, and to avoid mis-representing the case or arguments of our opponents. We should not, moreover, condemn those who hold opposing views. He suggested that if we put forward unconventional views, we need to take care of the language we use so as not to deter our audience. We owe respect to those who do not mis-represent their opponents. For Mill, this is the `real morality of public discussion'[12]. Mill was aware, however, that the force of an opinion is often determined by the context within which it is expressed. There is often, running through Mill's account, the assumption that divergent views of life will be exchanged according to some civilised code covering intellectual debate. When he wants to take account of settings other than this, he talks about the need to have at least some restrictions upon `freedom of action'.

Mill illustrated the difference between freedom of speech and freedom of action with his so-called `harm principle'. He claimed that individuals should have freedom from interference as long as their actions do not put others at risk, and that those acts which `without justifiable cause, do harm to others' require the `active interference of mankind'[13]. There was, he claimed, a difference between freedom of speech and freedom of action. Using the example of a corn dealer, he said that although it was perfectly legitimate to publish articles claiming that corn dealers were starving the poor, a demonstration against corn dealers which took place outside the home of a corn dealer should be restricted. He pointed out, however, that such

---

[11] Mill, *On Liberty*, p44.
[12] Mill, *On Liberty*, pp54-55.
[13] Mill, *On Liberty*, p56.

restrictions should only be applied if an action causes or threatens harm to somebody else; people should not be restricted simply because their actions lead to the 'displeasure' of others. These limits would be beneficial in two main ways. Firstly, it would allow other people to develop. Secondly, by restricting the selfish part of our natures, each of us might experience the development of our social natures[14].

Mill's defence of freedom of speech takes into account both freedom and responsibility. He sees freedom of speech as one of our most fundamental rights. At first sight, it seems very much like a right which serves primarily the interest of the individual. It encourages self development by allowing us to uncover truths, test our views, and avoid becoming dogmatic and intellectually stale. Mill's theory, however, also contains a heavy emphasis upon our social responsibilities. We have a duty or responsibility (rather than a right) to be tolerant of others. We have no right to limit what others can think, and we owe respect to our intellectual opponents. This tolerance has social implications for its is necessary for the maintenance of an open society, it helps to build an intellectual climate in which others can grow, and is necessary for social progress. Although Mill believed that it was wrong to suppress opinions simply because they cause displeasure, he was willing to allow the state to prevent the expression of opinions if the context in which they were expressed was likely to cause harm to others. This restriction is not necessarily a bad thing. Mill saw that some restrictions on freedom of expression could benefit society by allowing others to develop and through nurturing our social natures. Mill's liberal defence of freedom of speech thus recognises the importance of cultivating a sense of social responsibility.

The liberal defence of freedom of speech is sometimes used by the intelligentsia to justify the expression of all views regardless of their social consequences. One of the most recent and revealing examples was furnished by the controversy surrounding the publication of Salman Rushdie's *The Satanic Verses* in 1988. This book was

---

[14] Mill, *On Liberty,* p56 and p63.

thought to slander the name of the prophet Mohammed and denigrate the Islamic faith. Mohammed is presented as a businessman who makes deals with the archangel and God. He is described as a `smart bastard' and a womaniser, his assistants are portrayed as clowns, his wives as whores, and the *Koran* is reduced to a rule book of toiletry habits and sexual positions[15]. Rushdie defends his work on the grounds of freedom of expression. He claimed that freedom of expression ceases to exist unless we have the `freedom to offend' and the `freedom to challenge'. He pointed out that he was not the instigator of racism and violence. Although these were the tactics of some of his critics rather than his supporters, these people still deserved the same right to express their views[16]. For many of his critics, however, freedom of speech is not an end in itself. It has been argued that Rushdie has abused this right and that it is a mere smoke screen to conceal the more sinister motives prompting the publication of *The Satanic Verses*. Furthermore, it is clear that Rushdie's defence of his work fails to take into account the importance of social responsibility. It is this omission that angered some of his conservative and socialist critics.

Conservatives have a reputation for being some of the harshest advocates of censorship. Andrew Heywood believes that this is an important feature of the Conservative ideology. He claims that many conservatives regard religion as a social cement. They are therefore critical of leaving moral questions to the free choice of the individual. Society has to uphold its most cherished beliefs, and protect them through censorship. Conservatives believe that `... what people watch on television or read in books should be subject to the guidance of laws because society must be protected against immorality'[17]. This means that established moral values are imposed on society in the interests of social stability and moral unity.

---

[15] B. Parekh, `The Rushdie Affair: Research Agenda for Political Philosophy', *Political Studies*, Vol XXXV111, 1990, pp695-709.

[16] S. Rushdie, `In Good Faith', *Independent on Sunday*, 4.12.1990.

[17] A. Heywood, *Political Ideologies*, Macmillan: London, 1992, p63.

A conservative critique of Rushdie can be found in Richard Webster's *A Brief History of Blasphemy*. Webster believes that defending Rushdie's work on the grounds of freedom of expression is dangerous, and that freedom is not necessarily good for democracy. Indeed, democracy is based upon the 'selective deprivation of freedom'. He doubts whether liberals are really fighting for freedom and suspects that they are attempting to enforce their own values on society and declare that other cultures (and Gods) are inferior. Liberals are accused of being too zealous in promoting freedom of expression, and of not paying enough attention to what is actually being expressed. This amounts to secular fundamentalism, and is at least as dangerous as religious fundamentalism. It can, indeed, lead directly to the development of an amoral society[18].

Webster argues that artists and writers must take responsibility for what they produce. They must, above all, learn to discriminate between evil restraints which should be attacked, and those which are necessary for the sake of decency and toleration. Those involved in the communication of ideas have broader civic and moral responsibilities. Freedom of expression is not a sufficient justification for abandoning these responsibilities. The law must, he argued, restrain insulting and provocative behaviour. The interests of public order means that freedom of expression must sometimes be curtailed. Words can hurt and provoke violence. If we want the freedom to express our views we must be aware of our broader social responsibilities. Webster believes that the demand for unconditional freedom of speech should be abandoned[19].

Webster's argument rests upon a fairly conservative view of society. He believes that liberals over-estimate the importance of freedom, and is condemning of writers who fail to write in a responsible manner. There is, in Webster's account, very little regard for freedom. He believes that freedom must be curtailed in the interests of democracy, morality, decency, and public order. The right

---

[18] R. Webster, *A Brief History of Blasphemy*, Orwell Press: Suffolk, 1990, pp 47-48, 53-55, 59-61.
[19] Webster, *A Brief History of Blasphemy*, pp 62-63 and p129.

to freedom of speech is thought to be less important than the social implications of what is being said. Webster's theory of social responsibility thus rests firmly on moral foundations. Whereas Mill claims that we have a responsibility to be tolerant and to contribute towards the progress of civilisation, Webster believes in preserving what is 'good' from the questionable motives of irresponsible writers. His argument would tend to suggest that liberalism is incapable of providing an intellectual framework in which freedom and responsibility are balanced harmoniously. Too much damage is thought to be caused in the name of freedom for it to be reconciled with an adequate appreciation of social responsibilities. In true conservative fashion, he argues that our social responsibilities must be given precedence over any rights we feel that we have to freedom and to freedom of speech.

Many writers in the socialist tradition also harbour severe doubts about the fundamental importance of liberal tolerance and free speech. Herbert Marcuse, for example, has argued that the liberal view of free speech is too indiscriminate, and that the right to free speech should not be used to 'protect false words and wrong deeds'. Freedom of speech should not be given to those who pose a threat to humanity. It is in no way an end in itself, and should only be valued to the extent that it contributes towards economic, social and personal freedom. Marcuse believed that we live in a society of 'total administration' and 'indoctrination'. Liberal assumptions concerning free expression are rendered meaningless in a system of centralised economic and political power. Our views are created for us. We can express dissenting views, but they are evaluated without reflection by the dominant conservative majority. Discussion thus loses its liberating force. The state sets the frame of reference within which we think and discuss. This power is backed by the state using police, prisons and mental institutions[20]. Under the existing capitalist system, therefore, tolerance and free speech are mere facades; designed to conceal vested interests and perpetuate gross inequalities. For this

---

[20] H. Marcuse, 'Repressive Tolerance', pp106-117 in R. Wolff, B. Moore and H. Marcuse, *A Critique of Pure Tolerance*, Cape: London, 1969.

reason he felt justified in abandoning complete toleration of all opinion.

Socialist reservations about freedom of speech can be seen in Bhikhu Parekh's critique of Salman Rushdie. Parekh looks less at the moral order of society, and more at the elitism ingrained in the liberal defence of free speech. He has argued that freedom of speech should not be defended on absolutist grounds but should be seen in terms of the views that are being expressed., and that freedom of speech is not an end in itself but `... needs to be reconciled with such other values as avoidance of needless suffering, social harmony, protection of the weak, truthfulness in the public realm, and the self- respect and dignity of individuals and groups'[21]. Parekh is critical of Rushdie's arrogance. Rushdie approaches the issue of freedom of speech from a writer's perspective, and seems to assume that what is good for him is also good for society. Parekh believes that this is, in part, a problem with the liberal creed. Liberalism assumes that freedom of speech is good in itself, and that its opponents are in some way barbarous or ignorant. This stems from the vested interests of writers and not from any impartial judgement. Parekh is not generally in favour of the government banning creative writing, but emphasises our right to express our own outrage against irresponsible or inflammatory works. In his view, a writer's freedom of expression should not be given precedence over the individual and collective social respect of other citizens[22].

Parekh claims that the liberal defence of freedom of speech has some serious shortcomings. He feels that it is far too elitist in its assumption that what is good for the intellectual community is necessarily good for other members of society. In Parekh's view, if we are to defend freedom of speech it should be from a communal rather than intellectual perspective. Freedom of speech can be

---

[21]   B. Parekh, `The Rushdie Affair and the British Press: Some Salutary Lessons', p74 in Parekh (ed), *Free Speech*, Commission for Racial Equality: London, 1990, pp 59-78.
[22]   Parekh, `The Rushdie Affair: Research Agenda for Political Philosophy', p707.

defended in democratic terms `... that is, in terms of the vital moral and cultural interests of the community as a whole, or else it will remain dangerously precarious'[23]. For Parekh and others, therefore, the rights of the individual to express him or herself must be balanced against the rights of the community. The freedoms we have must be balanced against our social responsibilities.

Socialists tend to view social responsibility in terms of what is good for humanity or for the community, rather than in terms of what is good for the moral framework of society. For Marcuse, freedom is an illusion created by the bourgeois state to protect itself, and freedom of speech is considered of less importance than other economic, social and personal freedoms. Writers have a responsibility to further the interests of humanity. Nothing of value can be gained from defending the right to freedom of speech if what is said results in human suffering. Parekh adopts a similar, though by no means identical, approach. He too argues that freedom of speech should not be seen as an end in itself, and adds that it smacks of elitism to argue otherwise. Although he is against state censorship, he believes that writers have broad social responsibilities and that what they write should aim to avoid causing harm, protect the weak in society, and help to maintain the self respect of individuals and groups. Although an advocate of freedom of speech, he is adamant that this right should in no way detract from our social responsibilities.

To say that we have social responsibilities does not mean that freedom of speech should not be valued. State censorship is clearly at odds with freedom of speech. It allows the individual to speak up to a point, then silences all dissident opinion. From a liberal perspective, this cannot be justified unless it can be proved that the context in which these views are expressed will cause harm to others. Equipping the state with the power to censor is dangerous to freedom and democracy, and does little to allow us to develop a sense of social responsibility. Conservative critics will no doubt point out that the state only intervenes when a person ignores these responsibilities.

---

[23]   Parekh, `The Rushdie Affair: Research Agenda for Political Philosophy', p708.

But such legal remedies are punitive rather than educative. A responsible citizenry is not created by depriving people of rights, but by encouraging people to use these rights wisely. This does not rely upon the state, but upon the citizen recognising his or her responsibility to the community.

Freedom of the press

Freedom of the press is often regarded as an essential element of a democratic society. A free press should exist to monitor the activities of the government, keep the public informed and give the public a platform from which to express its views. It has often been argued that Britain derives considerable strength and vitality from its long history of having a relatively free press. William Pitt remarked in the late eighteenth century that England had taught Europe that the foundation of true greatness lay in the freedom of the press and other civil liberties. Hegel praised the free press for the strength it gave to Britain. Voltaire congratulated it for encouraging people to think, and Montesquieu considered it an essential tool in undermining despotism and allowing Britain to develop into a modern society[24]. Freedom of the press was not guaranteed by constitutional principles, nor granted by the state to further the cause of democracy. The freedom derived from the demands of liberals, and the pragmatic good sense of conservatives coupled with the transforming influence of the competitive market.

Liberals tend to regard a free media as essential to guarantee that the state does in no way abridge our civil rights. Demands for a free press featured in many tracts written during the civil war of the seventeenth century. These tracts included the writings of Henry Burton, Henry Robinson, William Walwym and John Milton. Milton, whose reputation has survived long after his contemporaries, believed that a free press was necessary to allow people the freedom to think and to opt for a Christian life. Individuals must be allowed to choose

---

[24]   See J. Keane, *The Media and Democracy*, Polity/Blackwell: Cambridge, 1991 (1994 edition), p27.

between good and evil, rather than be passive recipients of what censors deem to be in their best interests. Although an advocate of a free press, he did believe that the state must maintain the power to punish those who abuse the right of free expression and he believed that it was generally self defeating to be tolerant of the intolerant[25].

Liberals continued to campaign for a free press during the eighteenth and nineteenth centuries. Matthew Tindal, for example, made a case for a free press during the eighteenth century on the grounds of natural rights. He claimed that we have a natural right to judge between what is good and evil, and to determine our own religious views. Governments should not interfere with the natural rights of individuals, and a free press is essential to prevent the government usurping these rights[26]. By the nineteenth century, the political system was changing rapidly, and many believed that freedom of the press was necessary to keep an eye on those with power. Jeremy Bentham, for example, claimed that in order to ensure that the government acts in the best interests of the community, a system of representative democracy is needed in which there is universal suffrage, annual elections, and secret ballot. Bentham believed freedom of speech and a free press were essential to safeguard this system. The free press is necessary to keep the government in check, to inform the public of any wrongdoing and to counteract corruption. Under no circumstances should the government determine which views should be published or suppressed. Such a government would be despotic. Thus, for Bentham, freedom of speech and of the press was essential for the maintenance of good government[27].

Liberals and radicals alike have always had to fight against the state assuming control over the press. The state has used a variety of methods to suppress the free flow of information. Britain has no written constitution which guarantees freedom of the press, and the

---

[25] Keane, *The Media and Democracy*, pp11-13.

[26] Keane, *The Media and Democracy*, pp13-15.

[27] G. Williams, *Political Theory in Retrospect*, Edward Elgar: Aldershot, 1991, p114.

British state has long been aware that the press could pose a threat to the existing power structure. The state assumed direct control over what was printed during the sixteenth century. Henry V111 banned the use of 'naughty and lewd words', and the Archbishop of Canterbury acted as a pre-publication censor. Censorship collapsed during the Civil War, but was restored again in 1660 (with the restoration of the monarchy) and remained in place until 1694. The final abolition of direct state censorship came about because the system was unable to deal with the increasing amount being published, and this gave rise to the publication of daily newspapers, starting with the *Daily Courant* in 1702[28].

This did not mean that the state no longer had any interest in controlling the press. In 1712, the state introduced taxes on the press in an attempt to confine access to news to those who could afford it. This tax was increased progressively throughout the eighteenth century. The state continued to exert influence also by providing funds and giving preferential treatment to those papers who supported a particular government. It was not until the early nineteenth century, when newspapers began to attract more advertisers, that the press were able to loosen the bonds of state patronage. The so-called 'stamp duty' provides a classic illustration of how attempts to suppress information can backfire. The declared aim of the stamp duty was to ensure that papers were prosperous enough to pay libel fines. Lord Castelereagh admitted in parliament, however, that it would ensure that '... persons exercising the power of the press should be men of some respectability and property'[29]. In the early nineteenth century, however, a group of radical papers refused to pay the tax. By 1836, there was an estimated 560 'unstamped' papers in Britain. These papers aimed to educate the working class. Middle class papers

---

[28] Keane, *The Media and Democracy*, p9, and J. Eldridge, J. Kitzinger and K. Williams, *The Mass Media Power in Modern Britain*, Oxford University Press: Oxford, 1997, p19. See also pp18-19.

[29] Lord Castlereagh cited in J. Curran, 'Press History' p12 in J. Curran and J. Seaton, *Power Without Responsibility*, Routledge: London, 1997, pp5-108.

were unable to compete, so the state abandoned the tax in an attempt to reduce the appeal of the radical press.

The actions of the radical papers forced disgruntled Tories to call for the abolition of the stamp duty. They argued that the stamp duty did nothing to prevent the radicals spreading their views, and that the stamp duty should be repealed so that the 'respectable' papers could reach a wider audience in their campaigns against the spread of radicalism and the trade union movement. According to Curran, the parliamentary campaigners for a free press were not motivated by libertarian principles but by `... the need for a more positive approach to political indoctrination'[30]. This move proved to be a success. The stamp duty was abolished in 1855, and newspapers were free to compete by increasing their advertising revenue and by reducing their cover prices. The radical press suffered under these conditions because advertisers preferred to do business with those papers which aimed at more affluent sections of society. The radical press went into decline and was eventually driven out of the market[31].

The fiasco over the stamp duty effectively transformed conservative views towards the free press. During the late eighteenth and early nineteenth centuries, many leading conservative theorists spoke out against freedom of the press. Edmund Burke thought that the press would be used to undermine the moral fabric of society. Windam felt that it was inclined to inject poison into the body politic, and Southey even supported flogging, hanging or transporting to the colonies for leaders of the radical press because they were effectively encouraging sedition amongst the lower orders of society[32]. What these theorists failed to take into account is that the use of oppressive methods will rarely do anything in the long run to secure the defeat of radical ideas and movements. It is far more likely that exerting state power in this way will provoke a radical response and discredit the democratic credentials of the modern state.

---

[30] Curran, `Press History', p23.

[31] Negrine, *Politics and the Mass Media in Britain*, p41, Eldridge, Kitzinger and Williams, *The Mass Media Power in Modern Britain*, pp20-21.

[32] See Keane, *The Media and Democracy*, p34.

Conservatives eventually realised that the radical press could be weakened by enlisting the support of advertisers and subjecting it to the rigours of the market.

Although formal links between the press and the state were undermined by the mid-nineteenth century, political parties found it necessary to court the press for favourable coverage and support. The mid-Victorian press thus became increasingly partisan. There was freedom of the press only to the extent that state control had been loosened and there was a choice of political perspectives in the market. All national dailies were allied to either the Liberal or the Conservative Party, and during the latter half of the nineteenth century an increasing number of newspaper owners became actively involved in politics. Between 1892 and 1910, there were between 20 and 30 MPs who owned newspapers[33]. The introduction of commercial pressure also had a dramatic effect on the content of newspapers. In the mid-late nineteenth century there was a gradual shift away from in-depth political coverage. Old style `principled journalism' gave way to a more populist style, lengthy commentaries were replaced by brief stories, and there was a marked decline in political coverage. No longer could key ministers expect to see their speeches in full. Shortened summaries were included in the papers, alongside increasingly sensational news and coverage of sports. Papers like the *News of the World* (established in 1843), deliberately aimed to please as many people as possible. According to Ralph Negrine, this change of style was reflected in the expectations that newspapers had of their readers. Readers were treated as intellectually passive, and as people who were more interested in elevating their own status than in cultivating wisdom[34].

The British press at the end of the nineteenth century was far from that envisaged by the early campaigners for a free press. Those who campaigned for a free press did so in the belief that it was necessary for democracy, essential for monitoring the activities of the

---

[33] Negrine, *Politics and the Mass Media in Britain*, p44. See also: pp42-44.

[34] Negrine, *Politics and the Mass Media in Britain*, pp45-46, and Curran, `Press History', pp29-30.

government and consistent with freedom of conscience and freedom of speech. The conservative establishment resisted the extension of freedom, and attempted to maintain the established order through censorship and taxation. Both policies proved unsuccessful because of the administrative nightmare they created and because of the non-compliance of radical sections of society. By the mid nineteenth century, the British press was free from overt state control but subject to the pulls and strains of the market. The radicals were unable to compete with the respectable press because they were effectively deprived of sufficient advertising revenue. The press increasingly provided people with entertainment and diversion, and paid far less attention to the political system. Britain had a free press, but one less mindful of its social responsibilities.

Controlling the Media

The British press has not always been spurred on by the highest of motives in its fight for freedom. During the seventeenth and eighteenth centuries, the press in Britain gained a reputation for spreading scandal. Demands were made for tight censorship because the newspapers were devoid of serious news and concentrated far too much upon `... murders and robberies, and rape and incest, and bestiality and sodomy, and sacrilege, and incendiary letters and forgeries, and executions and duels, and suicides ...'[35]. The spread of sensational reporting in the nineteenth century prompted John Stuart Mill to describe journalism as `... the vilest and most degrading of all trades because more affectation and hypocrisy and more subservience to the baser feelings of others are necessary for carrying it on than for any other trade from that of brothel keepers upwards'[36]. The spread of popular journalism increased the sensationalist character of news reporting. The so-called tabloids aim to entertain and do relatively little to inform the public on political matters, or play an active and

---

[35] *News and Newswriters* cited in R. Snoddy, *The Good, the Bad and the Unacceptable*, Faber and Faber: London, 1992 (1993 edition), p21
[36] J.S. Mill cited in Snoddy, *The Good, the Bad and the Unacceptable*, p21.

intentional role in fortifying democracy. This is the prerogative of a free but not of a responsible press.

The contemporary British media have come in for a lot of criticism for sacrificing principle to increase their share of the market. In July 1991, John Birt (at that time the Director-General of the BBC) claimed that ethical standards in the British media were slipping, and that the poor behaviour of some sections of the media was serving to undermine arguments for greater freedom of information and for less secrecy in British government. He complained, in particular, about the way that the media invaded the privacy of individuals without regard for what was in the interests of the public to know, and its disregard for the `standards of good taste and of decency'[37]. Other critics were more explicit in their views on the tabloids. In 1988, Lord Cudlipp (the former editor of the *Sunday Pictorial*) complained that the tabloids had reduced international news to insulting foreigners, had sacrificed a basic right to privacy in the interests of profit, and had pushed aside serious news for `... a panting seven day and night news service for voyeurs, the massage parlour relaxations of polo players and the exclusive definitive autobiographies of kiss-and-tell nymphets aged eighteen and a half'[38]. The same kind of criticisms were directed at the press by the Home Office minister David Mellor in 1989. He claimed that he was disgusted by press intrusion into the private lives of individuals, and argued that the press had to sort itself out or face the possibility of government restraint. He acknowledged that the government was reluctant to impose restraints; knowing that a free press was `... one of the foundation stones of a free society'[39].

Although the modern British state is reluctant to undermine the freedom of the media, it still looks for ways to control their activities. It has a number of legal tools which can be used. Civil servants, for example, are subject to over 100 different regulations which prevent

---

[37] John Birt (1991) cited in Snoddy, *The Good, the Bad and the Unacceptable*, p12.

[38] Lord Cudlipp cited in Snoddy, *The Good, the Bad and the Unacceptable*, p12.

[39] Snoddy, *The Good, the Bad and the Unacceptable*, p101.

them from providing the media with information. The press is limited by the Contempt of Court Act (1981) which places limits upon what it can say about trials, and even the proceedings of new water authorities take place without press scrutiny as a result of the 1983 Water Act[40]. The press is also restricted by criminal legislation on official secrets, sedition, obscenity, and blasphemy, and by civil laws of libel. Breach of confidence is sometimes used against the media. This began as a way to protect trade secrets, but has been extended to cover any information imparted in confidence. It has been used quite effectively in recent times to gag the press. Robert Maxwell managed to get a High Court injunction to prevent reports that his business empire was using 'dubious accounting devices'. The law of confidence was also used against Peter Wright's publication *Spycatcher*. This injunction was served on the *Guardian*, the *Observer* and the *Sunday Times* for repeating some of Wright's allegations about the activities of the British secret service[41]. According to Belsey and Chadwick, the judiciary in Britain is essentially unsympathetic to the idea of a free press and is willing to implement gagging injunctions against the press. This would not be possible under the American system of law[42].

Broadcasting is likewise subject to regulation. The Secretary of State has the power to prevent the broadcast of a particular programme, or programmes on a particular issue. Of particular importance is the regulatory functions of the Independent Television Commission, the Broadcasting Standards Council, the Radio Authority and the Broadcasting Complaints Commission. Although their functions overlap to some extent, each body has its own agenda. The Broadcasting Complaints Commission, for instance, looks into

---

[40] C. Lacey and D. Longman, *The Press as Public Educator*, University of Luton Press: Luton, 1997, p22.

[41] J. Petley, 'The Regulation of Media Content' pp147-148 in J. Stokes and A. Reading (eds), *The Media in Britain*, Macmillan: Houndmills, 1999, pp143-157.

[42] A. Belsey and R. Chadwick, 'Ethics and Politics of the Media', p6 in A. Belsey and R. Chadwick (eds), *Ethical Issues in Journalism and the Media*, Routledge: London, 1992, pp1-14.

accusations of inaccuracy, unfairness and intrusions into privacy. The Broadcasting Standards Council, on the other hand, deals with matters of decency, sex and violence. It argues that broadcasting must be scrutinised more than the press because television images have a greater effect upon the audience than those in the press and because there is the fear that violent images can blunt our sensibilities[43].

Although the British state certainly has legal methods to control the media, it has tended to favour a system of self-regulation. The state periodically sets up commissions to deal with the media. In 1990, for example, The Committee on Privacy and Related Matters was set up to investigate invasions of privacy by the press. The committee looked at the importance of protecting private life (matters relating to health, home and personal relationships) from media intrusion. The committee was formed following the failure of John Browne's Privacy Bill of 1989. Browne, the Conservative MP for Winchester, had argued that there needed to be a legal right to privacy. He failed, however, to gain enough support for a second reading of his bill (he got 98 of the 100 MPs needed) but the government, aware of pressure to curb the press, set up the Calcutt Committee to establish a system of self-regulation. The committee consisted of Sir David Calcutt QC, David Eady (a lawyer), John Spencer (a law lecturer at Cambridge University), Simon Jenkins (a columnist with the *Sunday Times*), Sheila Black (a businesswoman and former journalist), John Cartwright (Social Democratic Party MP for Woolwich), and Professor John Last (Director of the Charities Trust)[44].

The Calcutt Committee was regarded as a distinct threat by influential sections of the British media. Robert Maxwell (the publisher of Mirror Group Newspapers) and Kelvin Mackenzie (editor of the *Sun*) told the committee that newspapers had already started to reform themselves. Mackenzie claimed, indeed, that his publisher

---

[43]   Petley, 'The Regulation of Media Content', p149, Belsey and Chadwick, 'Ethics and politics of the media', p7, N. Harris, 'Codes of Conduct for Journalists', p64 in A. Belsey and R. Chadwick (eds), *Ethical Issues in Journalism and the Media*, Routledge: London, 1992, pp62-76.
[44]   Snoddy, *The Good, the Bad and the Unacceptable*, pp95-97.

(Rupert Murdoch) had forced him to change his behaviour and that he was responding, at least in part, to public pressure[45]. The Calcutt Committee was also criticised by some sections of the broadsheet market. The *Daily Telegraph* argued that the Calcutt proposals posed a threat to the freedom of the press and that it was `... a bitter price to pay for the behaviour of certain irresponsible newspaper proprietors'[46]. Conrad Black, the owner of the *Telegraph*, claimed that it was wrong and offensive for parliament to threaten the press with further controls and to set up a commission to monitor the activities of the press. He said that he accepted that it is `... desirable to improve the standards of the lower echelons of the British press, but this isn't the way to do it'[47]. This view had some support from the academic community. Professor David Flint, chair of the Australian Press Council, said that it was an unjustified attack upon freedom of speech and freedom of the press and that `... this series of assaults, this intimidation of a free press and indirectly a free people, is justified (in the government's eyes) by the actions of a minority of mavericks'[48].

The Calcutt Committee did not pose a significant threat to the freedom of the press. The committee claimed that it found no evidence to suggest that the press was becoming more intrusive into the private lives of individuals. Whilst it believed that a privacy law would be ill-advised, it claimed that something had to be done to curb excessively intrusive behaviour by members of the media. It claimed that a right to privacy could include protection against the publication of inaccurate personal material, embarrassing personal material (regardless of whether it's true), photographs taken without consent and physical intrusion. These rather broad categories were amended by Sir David Calcutt (the committee's chair) and published in 1992. The Calcutt Committee argued that new criminal offences should be

---

[45] Snoddy, *The Good, the Bad and the Unacceptable*, pp101-102.
[46] The *Telegraph* cited in Snoddy, *The Good, the Bad and the Unacceptable*, p105.
[47] Conrad Black cited in Snoddy, *The Good, the Bad and the Unacceptable*, p129.
[48] David Flint cited in Snoddy, *The Good, the Bad and the Unacceptable*, p107.

formulated to deal with the press entering private property, using surveillance devices to spy on people whilst on private property, taking a photograph or recording the voice of people on private property whenever any of these are done without the consent of the person involved. These recommendations would apply to material that is later published, but not to its mere collection. According to David Feldman, they are `... too narrow to satisfy those who are concerned at the powers of the security service and investigative agencies, and too wide to be acceptable to those who regard the press as a principal guardian against corruption in public life'[49]. The Calcutt Committee argued that the Press Council needed to be replaced by a Press Complaints Commission (PCC) to supervise the formation of a code of practice for the newspaper industry. They would have 18 months to do something about limiting intrusions into the private lives of individuals. Failure to do so would result in the possibility of parliament formulating new privacy legislation[50].

The PCC Code of Practice aimed to provide `benchmarks' for the `highest professional and ethical standards'[51]. The code was designed as the `cornerstone of the system of self-regulation'. It was argued that this system could only work if people observed not only the details but also the spirit of the code. It was important, in particular, that the `... code should not be interpreted so narrowly as to compromise its commitment to respect the rights of the individual, nor so broadly that it prevents publication in the public interest'[52]. The PCC code aims to encourage a responsible press without doing anything to curtail the legitimate freedom of the press.

---

[49]   D. Feldman, *Civil Liberties and Human Rights in England and Wales*, Oxford University Press: Oxford, 1993, p388.
[50]   Belsey and Chadwick, `Ethics and Politics of the Media', p7, M. Cloonan, `The Press part 1', *Case Studies for Politics 10* , University of York, *pp5-6*, T. Welsh and W. Greenwood, *McNae's Essential Law for Journalists*, Butterworths: London, 1995 (13th edition) p273, Snoddy, *The Good, the Bad and the Unacceptable*, pp95-99 and 103-105.
[51]   `Code of Practice' p1, http://www.pcc.org.uk/complain/newcode.htm
[52]   `Code of Practice', p1.

The PCC Code of Practice stipulates a number of regulations which should guide journalists in the collection of material for their stories. It warns, in particular, against harassment, subterfuge and financial malpractice. It states that journalists must not seek to obtain material through 'intimidation, harassment or persistent pursuit' and that they must not persist in questioning or photographing people once they have been asked to desist. The code included special warnings against approaching people who are suffering from personal grief or shock, and that they must seek permission from a 'responsible executive' before entering 'hospitals or similar institutions'[53]. There is also a direct condemnation of harassing children. No child should be interviewed on subjects relating to child welfare without the consent of a parent, nor receive payment for information regarding child welfare. Children should, it claims, be free to attend school without press intrusion and should not be approached or interviewed without the permission of school authorities[54].

The PCC code is critical of subterfuge. It says that material should not be published if it is obtained using secret listening devices or wire tapping, though it also stated that subterfuge '... can be justified only in the public interest and only when material cannot be obtained by any other means'[55]. Financial malpractice is also highlighted. The PCC code states that journalists should not pay for material from witnesses in criminal proceedings, convicted or confessed criminals, nor the families, friends or colleagues of criminals. Once again, however, it states that this applies unless '... the material concerned ought to be published in the public interest and payment is necessary for this to be done'[56]. It also states that journalists should not profit from their knowledge of the financial market, nor write on specific financial matters in which they have a financial stake without declaring this interest to their editor[57].

---

[53] 'Code of Practice' (articles 4,5, 8 and 9), pp2-3.
[54] 'Code of Practice' (article 6), pp2-3.
[55] 'Code of Practice' (article 11. See also article 8), pp3-4.
[56] 'Code of Practice' (article 16), p4
[57] 'Code of Practice' (article 14), p4.

In addition to attempting to regulate how journalists gain their stories, the PCC code deals with some aspects of presenting the material. Journalists must, it claimed, be accurate, respect individual privacy, and be non-discriminatory. The code states that `inaccurate, misleading or distorted material' should not be published. Where mistakes are made, apologies must be published and the victim must have the right to reply. It was also important to distinguish between fact, comment and conjecture[58]. Journalists are called upon to respect the family life, home, health and correspondence of individuals, and publications `... will be expected to justify intrusions into any individual's private life without consent'[59]. Individuals can also expect not to be identified without consent as the friends or relatives of criminals or of those accused of criminal activity, and should not be identified as victims of sexual assaults. Children should not, under any circumstances, be identified in sex offence cases[60]. The press, according to the code, has to avoid discriminatory reporting. It should not make `... prejudicial or pejorative reference to a person's race, colour, religion, sex or sexual orientation or to any physical or mental illness or disability'[61]. Such descriptions should be avoided `... unless they are directly relevant to the story'[62]. The PCC code allows journalists to disregard many of these regulations if it can be shown that they are acting in the `public interest'. Its definition of the public interest includes exposing crimes, protecting public health and safety, and preventing the public from being misled. It is the responsibility of editors who publish material that transgresses the code of practice to explain to the PCC how their flouting of the code serves the public interest[63].

The aim of a code would be to identify certain unacceptable behaviour and remove journalists from a professional register if they break the code. Nigel Harris points out that codes of conduct are

[58] `Code of Practice' (articles 1 and 2), p2.
[59] `Code of Practice' (article 3), p2.
[60] `Code of Practice' (articles 7, 10 and 12), pp3-4.
[61] `Code of Practice' (article 13), p4.
[62] `Code of Practice' (article 13), p4.
[63] `Code of Practice', p1.

meant to benefit three main groups of people. The first is the readership of the paper or journal. If the code states that news items must be accurate and fair, then the readership would to some extent be protected from manipulation and they would be able to rely upon the information they receive[64]. The second group of beneficiaries are the sources of the journalist's information who could be protected under a breach of confidence clause. Finally, there are those who are being written about. A code of conduct could well demand that journalists have respect for the privacy of those about whom they are writing[65]. Harris is particularly critical of what he calls 'cheque-book journalism'. This is where journalists pay those intimately connected to a story for personal information about the main characters in a story. The PCC code argues that payment should not be made to criminals, but does not condemn using the revelations made by ex-employees or ex-spouses. Such sources may well exaggerate their versions to secure a higher fee[66]. Codes can also protect the journalist. Where journalists are under threat of persecution, it has been found that codes encourage solidarity within the journalist community. The Venezuelan Association of Journalists, for example, subscribe to a code which includes a clause stating that a journalist '... should give his support to his colleagues when they are being unjustly persecuted or are victims of acts violating the established law or from all other forms of provoked repression'[67]. It is notable that such protection for journalists is lacking in more 'liberal' regimes though, according to such commentators as Conrad Fink, journalists are in need of some protection from each other. This applies, in particular, to prohibiting plagiarism[68].

Harris points out, however, that the existence of a code could be counter-productive in duping the public into trusting the press more than is warranted. By prohibiting definite 'unethical' behaviour, it

---

[64] Harris, 'Code of conduct for journalists', p66.
[65] Harris, 'Codes of conduct for Journalists', pp66-67.
[66] Harris, 'Codes of conduct for journalists', p74.
[67] Venezuelan Association of Journalists cited in Harris, 'Codes of Conduct for Journalists', p73.
[68] Fink in Harris, 'Codes of conduct for journalists', p73.

could encourage journalists to look for loopholes. This could create the situation whereby journalists `... will come to treat as permissible anything that does not fit the precise specifications of unethical behaviour'[69]. He argued, in addition, that it made little sense to base a code upon abstract standards. Journalists are only likely to follow a code if it has its foundations in existing practice. He claims that existing codes tend to be too negative in nature in that they `... present lists of the types of action which are to be avoided, but say relatively little about what would constitute good practice and how it might be achieved'[70]. Belsey and Chadwick argue likewise that there is the problem of whether the code should be negative or positive; whether it should attempt to stamp out unethical behaviour or promote ethical conduct[71].

For many commentators, codes of conduct are too negative to shape good media practice and the solution lies in the field of media ethics. Codes can only prescribe rules, they cannot encourage a more thoughtful, responsible nor ethical media. Klaidman and Beauchamp have argued that written codes or rules are too cumbersome as a guide to good practice as the meanings of rules are often unclear and journalists are invariably working towards tight deadlines. It is more important, therefore, to cultivate virtue among journalists so that they are more likely to act in a responsible and ethical way[72]. Stephen Daniel claims that ethics is primarily concerned with the duties of individuals to themselves and to others. It is concerned with `self-enforced and self-legislated conduct' rather than following rules imposed from elsewhere. Media ethics is said to be concerned with both the personal responsibilities of the individual journalist to him or herself, and the social responsibilities of the journalist to the wider

---

[69] Harris, `Codes of conduct for journalists', p67.
[70] Harris, `Codes of conduct for journalists', p75.
[71] Belsey and Chadwick, `Ethics and politics of the media', pp9-10.
[72] E.D. Cohen (ed), *Philosophical Issues in Journalism*, OUP: New York, 1992, p36.

community. If a journalist behaves as a mere conduit for information, he or she is behaving neither as a responsible nor as an ethical being[73]. There are numerous ways of controlling the activities of the media. The state protects itself by using such things as the Official Secrets Act, whilst the rich and powerful tend to make use of the civil laws of libel and breach of confidence. The media have to operate within these legal limits. As the media can be punished under the existing legal system, it contributes in part to journalists censoring themselves (though not necessarily in the public interest). We do not have a completely free media nor responsible media. Failure to behave in a responsible manner allows the state to continue to maintain control over the information available to the public. One of the recurring arguments for responsible journalism is that unless the media reform themselves, it will allow the state to justify imposing further restrictions. The existing system of self-regulation prohibits certain behaviour and threatens to remove from the professional register those journalists who break the code of practice. By concentrating upon what journalists should not do, it does not necessarily encourage journalists to think about their broader social responsibilities. If journalists are to behave in a more responsible manner, they need to be willing at least to consider their role in the democratic process and to what extent they should serve the public interest.

Conclusion

The ideas of freedom and responsibility provide a framework to discuss the activities of the media. Freedom of the media is necessary for democracy, but only in so far as they assume their social responsibilities. When the media divert attention away from the political system and fail to keep the state in check, they cannot claim to be serving democracy. The media sometimes justify themselves by claiming that they give people what they want. This is a form of

---

[73] S. Daniel, 'Some conflicting assumptions of journalistic ethics' in E.D. Cohen (ed), *Philosophical Issues in Journalism*, OUP: New York, 1992, pp50-59.

consumer democracy, and has relatively little to do with the original aims of the free press. The media must, of course, be involved in entertainment; but not at the expense of their other social responsibilities. A free press and system of broadcasting are not necessarily good if they fail to monitor public life and reflect the diversity of modern society. State censorship would merely add to the problem for it threatens freedom of speech, protects the establishment and does little to encourage democratic debate. The choice is not between freedom and censorship, but between a media driven by commercial considerations and a media looking to nourish the democratic system.

2. Democracy and manipulation

It would be inappropriate to list the ways in which the media serve democracy without taking into account the way that those who work in the media are manipulated by the establishment. The media provide the citizen with news about the proceedings in parliament, new political initiatives and policies, and what these policies will mean to the audience. They can also alert readers and viewers to the pros and cons of new ventures, and to impending dangers. In the best of worlds, the media can provide the audience with a platform for active debate, and a place to air dissenting views. The citizens get to know their representatives through the media. The media can highlight the work of politicians, or thrill sections of the public with stories of sleaze. It would be wrong to see the media as mere neutral observers of the political system. The media are controlled by an elite minority with its own political agenda, and by the political machinery which affects the news we receive. The media can serve democracy, but are also bound by vested interests.

Democracy and the media

It is often thought that a free media and freedom of speech are essential for democracy. The argument suggests that democracy is threatened by state intervention in the affairs of the media. How can we insure that the public interest is served unless the media remain independent from the state ? The Press Commission, for example, said that a free press requires the absence of restraint and that this is `... essential to enable proprietors, editors and journalists to advance the public interest by publishing facts and opinions without which a democratic electorate cannot make responsible judgements'[1]. To say that a free press is essential for democracy does not necessarily mean

---

[1]   The Press Commission cited in J. O'Neill, `Journalism in the Market Place', p21, in A. Belsey and R. Chadwick (eds), *Ethical Issues in Journalism and the Media*, Routledge: London, 1992, pp15-32.

that British democracy is enhanced by the existing press. What it does mean is that placing restrictions upon the press can threaten both freedom of speech and the limited democracy we have in Britain. Liz Forgan, writing in *Index on Censorship*, has argued that there are too many restrictions placed upon the press in the name of `consumer protection'. Those who seek to control the activities of the media pose as defenders of individuals against an intrusive and abusive media. She argues that this constitutes `... an institutionalised erosion of the freedom of expression which should belong to us all'[2]. It is necessary, she claims, that we have a `baseline' to assess the demands of those who wish to censor; for whilst individuals might be gaining more protection, there is a distinct possibility that `... the wider public interest in a free press may be at risk'[3]. Establishing such a baseline would seem to be a legitimate area of concern for social and political theorists.

The first responsibility of a free press would be to monitor the activities of the state. To act as a kind of watchdog, serving the public interest and exposing political corruption. The British state exists to serve the interests of the British people, though it is apt to be captured by sections of the community and used to further the particular interests of the few rather than the general interest of the many. This, it could be argued, is the reality of politics. It is the responsibility of the media, however, to insure that those who control the state do not abuse their power. The media can act as a channel between the government and the electorate, and play an important role in `... articulating the agreed aims and values of society, helping society to adapt and change, and protecting the members of the public from wrongdoing or exploitation'[4]. This guardianship of the public interest requires the media to scrutinise the actions of the government, and expose corruption in public life.

James Curran has argued that the idea that the free media should serve as a `watchdog' is somewhat outdated. This idea was developed

---

[2] L. Forgan, `Trampling over Freedom', *Index on Censorship*, Volume 19, June/July 1990, p2.

[3] Forgan, `Trampling over Freedom', p2.

[4] Curran, `The Liberal Theory of Press Freedom', p286.

when the press was politicised and had a small circulation, prior to the development of a mass media dedicated to entertainment. The modern media does not spend a great deal of time scrutinising the state. The idea of the watchdog media also over-emphasises the oppressive powers of the state. Once again, this dates from a time when the state was manifestly unrepresentative. It is important to recognise that there are many centres of power and exploitation in contemporary society. The media are not free simply because they have freedom or autonomy from the state. The independence of the media is compromised continually by the interests of private media corporations which do relatively little to monitor the political system on behalf of the citizen[5]. If Curran is correct, it makes little sense to defend the freedom of the media on the grounds that the media act as watchdogs on our behalf, given that the bulk of the contemporary media does little to inform citizens about the political system.

The interests of democracy dictate that the media should have an educative role. The First Amendment of the American constitution, which guarantees freedom of speech and freedom of the press, was formulated to not only protect minority views but also to create a lively democratic system. Justice Brandeis claimed in his judgement in *Whitney v. California* (1927) that `... the greatest menace to freedom is an inert people; that public discussion is a political duty; and that this should be a fundamental principle of American government'[6]. The same would apply to any democratic system. Democracy relies upon the existence of an informed electorate to judge between political alternatives (at the very least), and to scrutinise those in power. The media must help to make politics accessible to the citizen, for democracy relies upon `... an open state in which people are allowed to participate in decision making, and are given access to the media, and other information networks through

[5] J. Curran, `Mass Media and Democracy Revisited', pp85-90 in J. Curran and M. Gurevitch (eds), *Mass Media and Society*, Arnold: London, 1996, pp81-115.
[6] Justice Brandeis cited in E. Barendt, *Freedom of Speech*, Clarendon: Oxford, 1985, p20.

which advocacy occurs[7]. Democracy relies upon an informed citizenry. It is essential that the media inform the electorate on public matters, offer opinions, suggest a range of political alternatives and provide a forum for debate. If the media assume their social responsibilities, they can fuel public debate.

A free media does not necessarily enliven the political system. There is a convincing argument that states that such media divert the public away from any involvement in politics, manipulate public opinion, and induce mass apathy amongst significant sections of the population. In 1807, William Cobbett claimed that the English press did not enlighten people, but sought to keep them in ignorance. He claimed that the press aimed to make slaves of people and that it was `... the most efficient instrument in the hands of all those who oppress or wish to oppress them'[8]. This line of argument has been restated in a variety of ways by radical social theorists during the twentieth century.

In his essay `The Industrialisation of the Mind', Hans Enzenberger addresses the aims and methods of what he refers to as the `mind industry' (the media and the film industry, in particular). He claims that the mind industry arose with the development of the modern democratic state. It presupposes that we have intellectual independence, yet seeks to deprive us of this independence. It's roots are economic. As capitalism develops, it requires a more sophisticated and educated work force. The ruling class are thus faced with a dilemma: The workers need to be educated, but in receiving this education, they become more conscious of their circumstances and thus pose a threat to the established order[9].

The mind industry exists to gain support for the existing order. Once people's bare material needs have been satisfied, it is likely that people will push for their human rights which, for Enzenberger, include the right to be free from exploitation. The ruling class must

[7] Hauser cited in B. McNair, *An Introduction to Political Communication*, Routledge: London, 1995, p22. See also p21.
[8] William Cobbett (1807) cited in Keane, *The Media and Democracy*, p32.
[9] H.M. Enzenberger, `The Industrialisation of the Mind', in *Raids and Reconstructions*, Pluto: London, 1976.

therefore find ways to conceal its exploitative activities and gain the compliance of the masses. It does this by attempting to control the minds of the people. He argues that we are becoming less aware of being exploited. We are subject not only to material exploitation but also to 'immaterial exploitation'. This has been achieved through censorship and direct state control of the mind industry, and has resulted in the 'immaterial pauperisation' of the many[10]. Enzenberger acknowledged that it is difficult for us to avoid being influenced by the mind industry, for it influences all areas of social life. The mind industry does, however, suffer from internal divisions. It is also caught in the contradiction that in order to exploit our mental powers, these powers must first be developed. Enzenberger believes intellectuals had a responsibility to use the media to undermine the existing power structure[11].

A similar argument has been put forward by Noam Chomsky and Edward Herman. Based upon their research into the media in the USA and Britain, they argue that economic and political inequalities allow some individuals to control the media. This power is used to 'filter' information with the aim of 'manufacturing consent'. They argue that we do not get news in its raw form. Instead, it is cleansed or filtered for political purposes. Elites determine what is newsworthy and how it is to be presented. They process information through a series of filters. What we receive depends upon who owns the media, the power of advertisers in determining the content of the media, ties between the media and the political system, and whether the news reinforces or detracts from the dominant ideology in society. The media are only liable to cover those stories which pass through this series of filters. These filters exist to tell the media what should and should not be reported. They assist the media in protecting their own interests, and the interests of the dominant economic and political elites[12].

---

[10] Enzenberger, 'The Industrialisation of the Mind', pp14-16.
[11] Enzenberger, 'The Industrialisation of the Mind', pp16-19.
[12] E. Herman and N. Chomsky, *Manufacturing Consent*, Vintage: London, 1994, ch1.

In the best of worlds, the media would not only act as guardian of the public interest but also provide a platform for political debate. It is argued that the reverse is too often the case, and that the media manipulate public opinion, induce apathy, and help to `manufacture consent' for the status quo. The media are said to filter information so as to create a compliant electorate; unaware of the true power of the media, fearful of radical political alternatives and relatively comfortable with the ideology of the ruling class. The most powerful propaganda is that which takes place at a covert level. Open support for a particular political alternative is less manipulative than bias that is concealed. News that has been made politically safe as a result of being filtered does little to scrutinise the system, nor does it stimulate radical debate. The slanted messages we receive from the media can be attributed to the elite ownership of the media, and to the relationship between the media and the political system.

Elite ownership and control

The media have their own interests and their own political agendas. This places severe limits on the type of contribution that the media can make to the democratic system. Chomsky and Herman point out that although in the USA that there were over 25,000 media organisations in 1986 (newspapers, magazines, T.V. and radio stations), the vast majority of these were very small and dependent upon national organisations for much of their news. This news was controlled by 24 `top tier' organisations, some of which controlled a variety of media. General Electric, for example, own RCA, NBC, Westinghouse and a variety of TV, cable and radio stations. In addition, it provides financial support to right wing think tanks like the American Enterprise Institute[13]

This media rely heavily upon advertising revenue, which allow newspapers in particular to be sold at under cost price. This is said to expose the press to the political influence of advertisers. Papers aiming at those of modest means have found it particularly difficult to

---

[13] Herman and Chomsky, *Manufacturing Consent*, pp4-5 and 12-13.

compete; for advertisers have less incentive to place their adverts in such papers. In Britain, for example, many of the `social democratic' papers (such as the *Daily Herald*, the *News_Chronicle*, and the *Sunday Citizen*) went out of business despite their high readership because this was not reflected in high advertising revenue. The *Daily Herald*, for example, had in its last year double the combined readership of the *Times*, the *Guardian* and the *Financial Times*. It had 8.1 % of the national circulation, but only 3.5 % of the advertising revenue. The fall of the *Daily Herald* and other similar papers did much to hasten the decline of the Labour Party[14].

In America, adapting television programmes to woo advertisers has become a fine art. The Client Audience Profile provides advertisers with information concerning the buying power of audiences and the most profitable advertising slot for their clients. Shows and networks are rated according to the audience they attract, and it is estimated that a 1 % loss in the ratings can amount to a loss of advertising revenue of $80 to $100 million a year. Advertisers will generally be sceptical of any network which is critical of corporate activities. Gulf and Western, for example, withdrew its advertising from WNET after it screened `Hungry for Profit' (1985) which criticised the exploitative role of multi-nationals in the developing world. Gulf and Western regarded this programme as `anti-business if not anti-American'[15]. Advertisers, in addition, prefer to support light entertainment programmes because they tend to believe that `serious complexities and disturbing controversies' disrupt the `buying mood'[16].

The centralised elite ownership of the national media in Britain has had a devastating effect upon the range of views we receive. A free press does not guarantee freedom of speech because editors and proprietors have the power to deny access to their pages. John O'Neill claims that freedom of the press does not lead to freedom of speech but to the power of some people to control the speech of others[17]. The press, in the majority of cases, is controlled by private

---

[14] Herman and Chomsky, *Manufacturing Consent,* pp14-15.
[15] Herman and Chomsky, *Manufacturing Consent,* p17.
[16] Herman and Chomsky, *Manufacturing Consent* ,p17.
[17] O'Neill, `Journalism in the market place', p16.

individuals who can act free of 'ethically significant boundaries'. Simply having a so-called free press is of limited value unless a fair range of people can gain access to the press. Those who own and control the press are in a privileged position, and can use this position to limit the views that are expressed. Minority ownership and control of the media prevents true freedom of the media. Lord Goodman, the chair of the Newspaper Publishers' Association, said that press freedom relied on '... the right of the man who controls the newspaper to say what he likes, no matter how perverse, absurd or cross-grained'[18]. Tom Baistow claims that it is virtually impossible for the press to fulfil its remit as watchdog for the public because the '... watchdogs have become press barons' poodles, yapping in support of their masters' views and commercial interests, barking against any threat to their undemocratic power'[19].

Economic and social elites gained incredible power over the British press during the early years of the twentieth century. One of the most formidable influences in the media was the Harmsworth family. Alfred Harmsworth (Lord Northcliffe) owned the *Daily Mail*, the *Times*, the *Weekly Dispatch*, and the *London Evening News*. Vere Harmsworth (Lord Rothermere) owed the *Daily Mirror*, the *Sunday Mail*, the *Sunday Pictorial*, the *Daily Record*, and the *Glasgow Evening News*. Their brother Lester Harmsworth controlled a series of local newspapers in the south of England[20]. These so-called press barons had considerable political power, and occasionally mounted overt political campaigns of their own. During the early 1930s, Lord Beaverbrook and Lord Rothermere challenged the government of Stanley Baldwin with their 'empire crusade'. This involved giving support to candidates in by-elections who promised to pursue a policy of imperial free trade, in direct opposition to official Conservative

---

[18]   Lord Goodman (1975) cited in A. White, 'Race, press freedom and the right of reply', p80 in P. Cohen and C. Gardner (eds), *It Aint Half Racist Mum*, Comedia: London, 1982, pp80-83.
[19]   Tom Baistow (1985) cited in Snoddy, *The Good, the Bad and the Unacceptable*, p13.
[20]   Eldridge, Kitzinger and Williams, *The Mass Media Power in Modern Britain*, pp27-28.

policy. Although they failed to over-turn government policy, they were criticised by the *Times* and by Stanley Baldwin for their lack of social responsibility[21]. In 1930, Baldwin attacked Beaverbrook and Rothermere for using their papers as instruments of propaganda and claimed that these newspapers owners wanted `... power; but power without responsibility - the prerogative of the harlot through the ages'[22].

In October 1946, a Royal Commission was set up by the Labour government to investigate the ownership and financing of the national press. The press was, at that time, under the control of the press barons Rothermere (the *Daily Mail*), Beaverbrook (the *Daily Express*), and Lord Kemsley (*Daily Sketch, Daily Graphic,* and the *Sunday Times*). The Labour MPs Hayden Davis and Michael Foot argued that an investigation was required because the freedom of the press and standards of journalism were being undermined by this elite control[23]. The Commission's report of 1949, however, did not stray from the view that freedom of the press could only rest upon a system of private enterprise. It argued that having the freedom to publish was necessary to produce a press which would reflect a diversity of views[24]. It was noted, however, that advertisers were having a detrimental effect upon the content of papers. In particular, they were said to exert pressure on newspapers not to include too much international news. This was thought to be `bad for business'. The Commission was unable to prove the existence of direct coercion by the business community, nor could it find conclusive proof that the owners were operating a blacklist which either excluded from their papers or minimised the importance of stories dealing with people they disliked[25].

James Curran argues that the press barons represented a continuation of earlier trends in the ownership of the press. Under

[21] Negrine, *Politics and the Mass Media in Britain*, pp48-49.
[22] Stanley Baldwin cited in Snoddy, *The Good, the Bad and the Unacceptable*, p78.
[23] Snoddy, *The Good, the Bad and the Unacceptable*, p76.
[24] Curran, `The Liberal Theory of Press Freedom', p288.
[25] Snoddy, *The Good, the Bad and the Unacceptable*, pp77-79

their guidance, the press did not on the whole become more propagandist. Rather, the press turned away from political parties and placed more emphasis upon entertainment. He argued that the press barons should not be evaluated according to whether any of their political campaigns had a direct effect upon the British people, but in terms of `... the way in which their papers provided cumulative support for conservative values and reinforced opposition, particularly among the middle class, to progressive change'[26]. The power of the press barons was intensely personal. It was power held by particular individuals who were willing to use their ownership of the press to further their own causes. Beaverbrook admitted to the Royal Commission of 1946, for example, that he ran the *Daily Express* with the sole purpose of `making propaganda' on behalf of important issues rather than in the interests of any particular political party[27]. This tendency for the press to remain under the ownership and control of an elite minority continued throughout the century. In the post-war period, ownership of the press has become increasingly concentrated into the hands of large corporations which use their power over the press and broadcasting in their attempts to undermine competitors and to dominate the markets in which they operate[28].

Those who own the press often exert influence upon the editorial policies and style of their papers. Victor Matthews, head of the *Express* group between 1977 and 1985, claimed that he gave his editors complete freedom as long as they followed his policies. He is famed for pushing his own views on his editors, and expecting his views to be reflected in editorials. It is said that he bullied Peter Grimsditch, his editor of the *Daily Star*, for criticising Mrs. Thatcher. He is reputed to have telephoned Grimsditch after reading proofs of an editorial which criticised the Thatcher government's first budget. He informed his editor that there were no poor in Britain. Grimsditch backed down and revised his copy[29].

---

[26] Curran, `Press History', p52. See also p42.
[27] Beaverbrook cited in Snoddy, *The Good, the Bad and the Unacceptable*, p78.
[28] Keane, *The Media and Democracy*, p72.
[29] Curran, `Press History', p56 and p75.

Perhaps the most powerful proprietor of modern times is Rupert Murdoch. He has been criticised by some of his editors for intervening too much in the internal workings of his papers. Harold Evans, the former editor of the *Times,* found Murdoch's intervention intolerable. Murdoch criticised Evans for his apparent hostility towards Mrs. Thatcher and for his interest in international news. Evans recalled that Murdoch was intolerant of the One Nation conservatives who argued that Mrs. Thatcher had abandoned her responsibility for the welfare of the people, and for any political views that were not overtly supportive of the Thatcher government. Murdoch is said to have been active in foisting his own right wing views on his editor. Evans was eventually replaced by Frank Giles and subsequently Andrew Neil, who was thought to be closer to Murdoch in politics and attitudes[30]. Evans, embittered by the experience, claimed that Murdoch uses his papers to spread right wing propaganda and to promote his own business interests. According to Evans, Murdoch is a `... cold-eyed manipulator who has shown a contempt for democracy and debate'[31].

This view of Murdoch is certainly not shared by all of his editors. David Montgomery, who edited both the *News of the World* and *Today* for Murdoch, claimed that Murdoch allowed him a great deal of editorial freedom. He admitted that he `toed the Tory line' at General Elections and that Murdoch would probably have intervened if he had started campaigning for Labour. The Murdoch group was also willing to tolerate Montgomery's brief flirtation with Green ideas[32]. Andrew Neil, likewise, found Murdoch to be a quite tolerant proprietor. Neil, the former editor of the *Sunday Times,* recalled how Murdoch was willing to permit Neil's support for Michael Heseltine in the Conservative leadership campaign of November 1990. Neil believed that this showed that `... proprietors concede a considerable amount of independence to editors and invest millions in their

---

[30] Curran, `Press History', p75 and Eldridge, Kitzinger and Williams, *The Mass Media Power in Modern Britain*, pp35-36.

[31] Harold Evans cited in Eldridge, Kitzinger and Williams, *The Mass Media Power in Modern Britain*, p40.

[32] Snoddy, *The Good, the Bad and the Unacceptable*, p127.

instincts and views with only one condition - circulation success'[33]. These recollections would tend to suggest that although Rupert Murdoch is far from the dictatorial ogre he is sometimes assumed to be, his political tolerance is limited to a relatively narrow range of ideas. He is motivated by what he considers to be good for the business community in general, and for his own business interests in particular. He does not strike even his most loyal supporters as somebody who is willing to stray too far from the principles of the free market.

It seems quite clear that editors have to choose between accepting the direction of their proprietors and fighting for editorial independence. Minor differences of opinion do not necessarily disrupt good working relations between owners and editors. Conrad Black, owner of the *Telegraph*, intervened in editorial policy on a narrow range of issues. He has been interested in international relations in general, and in Anglo-American relations in particular. This was shown, for example, in his criticisms of Max Hastings' handling of the US bombing of Libya in 1986, and in his trying to steer the *Telegraph* away from using the term 'Irangate' to suggest a scandal in Reagan's administration approached the magnitude of 'Watergate'. Hastings, however, did not expect to be independent from the wishes of Conrad Black[34]. The alternative approach is illustrated by Donald Trelford and his relations with Tiny Rowland. Trelford, the former editor of the *Observer*, preserved his editorial freedom against the business interests of Tiny Rowland, the owner of *Observer*. In April 1984, he wrote an article which exposed military atrocities in Zimbabwe. Rowland's Lonrho group had substantial investments in Zimbabwe, and Trelford was instructed to withdraw the article. Trelford, who had the support of his editorial staff, refused to withdraw the article and Rowland, fearing a prolonged scandal, was forced to back down[35].

---

[33]   Andrew Neil cited in B. McNair, *News and Journalism in the UK*, Routledge: London, 1994 (1996 edition), p45.

[34]   Snoddy, *The Good, the Bad and the Unacceptable*, pp130-131, and Curran, 'Press History', p88.

[35]   Curran, 'Press History', p86.

The elite ownership of the press is seen as a distinct problem by those drawn from the left of the political spectrum. Ralph Miliband pointed out in the early 1970s that `... those who own and control the capitalist mass media are most likely to be men whose ideological dispositions run from soundly conservative to utterly reactionary'[36]. Norman Angell argued that the owners of the press both manipulated public opinion to serve their own political agendas, and deprived the vast majority of the information they require to participate in the democratic process[37]. Murdoch and Golding have argued that the capitalist class control the production and distribution of ideas. The views of this class get constant publicity, they dominate the thinking of all subordinate classes and use this ideological domination to maintain class inequalities[38]. It is in this constant reinforcing of establishment views that the media help to dominate thinking and manipulate public opinion.

The elite ownership and control of the press limits its contribution to democracy. The elites help to establish a framework for thinking which marginalises radical opinion, excludes those who fall outside the acceptable framework, promotes a fairly conservative view of the world, and reduces publicity for political dissenters. Elites ensure that the press is not an open and democratic forum, but a relatively closed instrument for the minority to present their own interests as the general interest. The interests of big business and of the giants in the media world are no doubt compatible with the interests of some sections of society, but they in no way approach what can be construed as the general or public interest.

Politicians and the media

The assumption that the media monitor the political system on our behalf is unrealistic given the elite control of the press and the close

---

[36] Ralph Miliband cited in McNair, *News and Journalism in the UK*, p44.
[37] Norman Angell in Eldridge, Kitzinger, and Williams, *The Mass Media Power in Modern Britain*, p29.
[38] Murdoch and Golding summarised in Negrine, *Politics and the Mass Media in Britain*, p63.

relations between politicians and the media. The media rely upon the co-operation of those who frequent the corridors of power. Political elites provide the media with information and do all they can to determine the slant of the news we receive. Politicians are apt to view the media as tools to mobilise support, discredit their opponents and increase their own political power. This contrasts sharply with the view that the media are necessary to ensure that politicians remain accountable to the public for their views and activities.

Chomsky and Herman argue that government and large corporations exert power over the media by providing selective information. The government has direct links with the media through media lobbying of government officials and through the patronage offered by the media to former government officials. The media also need government support to assist in exporting their product. Diplomatic assistance is necessary for the media to be granted the right to bombard other cultures with their messages. The media also rely upon information provided by government press conferences. The Pentagon, for example, spends millions of dollars each year on its public information service. Information from the American government is important because it is regarded as accurate and thus helps the media to 'maintain the image of objectivity'. The media also rely upon information from large corporations. These corporations provide journalists with copies of speeches and reports, press conferences and photo opportunities. This effectively subsidises the media for it reduces the costs of collecting information. This close relationship sometimes makes the media reluctant to criticise too harshly the sources they value. These sources are in a position to 'flood the media' so as to swamp adverse publicity. The government can create a political agenda of its own by providing information on an issue so as to keep other stories off the front page[39].

Politicians in Britain have become increasingly skilful at manipulating the media. According to Channel Four's Jon Snow, democracy is under threat from a media which replaces real debate with sound bites and reduces politics to '... the more easily

---

[39] Herman and Chomsky, *Manufacturing Consent* ,p13, p19 and pp21-23.

communicated evidence of human frailty'[40]. Jeremy Paxman claims that he approaches political interviews thinking (or knowing) that his interviewees are lying to him[41]. Although politicians have learnt the art of using the media, this does not necessarily mean that it improves the quality of political life. Roger Bolton has noted that most political interviews serve no real purpose because politicians prepare for these interviews, and refuse to be drawn into any real political argument. This had led to the rise of aggressive journalistic practice to gain a response, yet it invariably fails to explore the complexities of issues[42]. The political presenter Nick Ross also argues that the ability of politicians to deal with the media has been transformed. They have become more skilled at public relations, and this has turned the general public against the parliamentary politics[43].

It could be argued that the media and politicians are increasingly involved in a game which deprives the vast majority of detailed knowledge and the will to engage in political activity. Although many sections of the media clearly have their own political agendas, it can also be said that the media are being blocked by the polished art of political communication. The Conservatives put a lot of energy into media presentation during the early 1980s. The 1983 Conservative Conference, for example, made use of the public relations talents of Harvey Thomas. He designed a stage set which looked like a giant grey battleship, and seated the Conservative front bench like conquering generals. This was the impression that the Conservatives wanted to give in the immediate aftermath of the Falklands War[44].

The Conservative government was, for a time, very successful at manipulating the media. Bernard Ingham, Mrs. Thatcher's press

---

[40] Jon Snow cited in B. McNair, 'Journalism, politics and public relations' p61, in M. Kieran (ed), *Media Ethics*, pp49-65.
[41] Paxman in Eldridge, Kitzinger and Williams, *The Mass Media Power in Modern Britain*, p117.
[42] Roger Bolton interviewed in *News and the Democratic Agenda*, BBC2, 13.03.1998
[43] Nick Ross interviewed in *News and the Democratic Agenda*.
[44] McNair, *An Introduction to Political Communication*, pp119-120.

44

secretary, pushed the interests not only of the Thatcher government, but also sought to gain support for Thatcher's ideas in the Conservative Party. He had a masterly grasp of the lobby system, which allows the government to brief journalists without being accountable for the story. This system allows the spokesperson to remain anonymous and preserve the 'quintessentially English atmosphere of a gentleman's club'[45]. This system was allegedly used to discredit those who fell out of favour with Thatcher. Its victims are said to include such people as John Biffen, Leon Brittan and Nigel Lawson[46]. It has been argued that the lobby system poses a threat to democracy. It allows politicians to manipulate journalists, and preserves the culture of secrecy that dominates British government. Some journalists have refused to participate in the charade. For a time during the 1980s, the *Independent* and the *Guardian* withdrew from the system in the hope that the system would change. Their withdrawal apparently did nothing to convince the powers that be to introduce a more open and democratic alternative[47]

The Labour Party learnt a lot from the Conservative manipulation of the media. In an attempt to fight against the ingrained Conservative bias in much of the national media[48], it devoted time and resources to develop the art of the 'spindoctor'. These spindoctors include Peter Mandelson and Alistair Campbell. Mandelson led the way when he set up the Shadow Communications Agency in 1985 to co-ordinate the public relations, advertising and marketing of the Labour Party. According to David Hughes, the political editor of the *Daily Mail*, Peter Mandelson did much to tighten up Labour's image in the media. Mandelson is said to know what is going on and has a good grasp of the 'chemistry of newspapers'[49]. Alistair Campbell has continued in this tradition of

---

[45] Robert Harris cited in McNair, *An Introduction to Political Communication*, p135.
[46] McNair, *An Introduction to Political Communication*, p136.
[47] McNair, *An Introduction to Political Communication*, p136.
[48] This will be explored in more detail in chapter three.
[49] David Hughes interviewed in *Have they got news for you*, BBC1, 30.09.1996

media management. He claims that his role involves ensuring that the most important points of party policy are communicated, and that a consistent position is presented. He is adamant that this in no way stifles debate'[50].

Spindoctors provide the press with information when ministers are not ready to go on record. The press have access to spindoctors in the lobby of parliament. It allows the press to gain information, but they are not allowed to quote directly[51]. According to the journalist Simon Heffer, the role of the spindoctor goes beyond that of a mere press officer. Whereas a press officer provides facts and background information, the spin doctor's role is to `... outline to journalists exactly what he feels the thrust of their story should be; it is to persuade them to accentuate the positive and ignore or at least play down the negative'[52]. Brian McNair claims that spin doctor's rely upon `... aggressive lobbying, accompanied by punitive action against dissenting journalists'[53]. The spindoctor seeks to control the flow and character of information published by the media. The spindoctor filters and purifies stories to maximise support and minimise damage to the party.

Spindoctors have an important role in diverting attention away from unfavourable publicity. During the height of Conservative splits over Europe, for example, John Major attacked some of the recipients of National Lottery grants. Spindoctors provided the press with a list of `unworthy' or `loony' winners of lottery grants[54]. Conservative spindoctors were also successful in diverting media attention away from the Conservative Party's poor performance in the local elections of 1990. Although the Conservative Party lost a significant number of seats in the local elections, Kenneth Baker emphasised how the Conservatives had managed to maintain control of some London

---

[50]   Alistair Campbell cited in McNair, `Journalism, politics and public relations', p56.

[51]   *Have they got news for you.*

[52]   Simon Heffer cited in McNair, `Journalism, politics and public relations' p55.

[53]   McNair, `Journalism, politics and public relations', p55.

[54]   *Have they got news for you*

boroughs. Brendan Bruce (the Conservative Party's Director of Communications 1989-1990), told Kenneth Baker to hold up the front pages of the *Sun* and *Daily Express*. The headlines of the *Sun* read `Kinnock Poll Axed'. The headline of the *Express* claimed that `Maggie Holds Labour'. A more truthful story, according to Bruce, would have had the headline `Labour Landslide in Local Elections'[55].

According to John Sergeant, the chief political correspondent at the BBC, opposition ministers are sometimes advised to ask deliberately boring questions during Prime Minister's Question Time so as to deprive the Prime Minister of headline stories. Tony Blair did this, for example, so as not to upstage a Labour press conference held earlier in the day[56]. Spindoctors are also reputed to use their position to discredit uncooperative MP's and colleagues. Clare Short, for example, described the spindoctors as `people in the dark'. Mandelson is said to have retaliated by saying that `... she's bitter, she needs a holiday'[57]. This behind the scenes approach to sourcing the media does little to create an open and accountable democratic system, and these practices have been condemned by the media and by some sections of the political community.

Political journalists have expressed concern about the rise of spindoctors. Michael Brunson of ITN claimed that spindoctors bully, and that this has to be resisted for if the other side see that bullying works, it will get out of control[58]. Alan Rusbridger of the *Guardian* said that it was right to be concerned about the rise of spindoctors and their attempt to control the political process. Particularly insidious is the spindoctor's use of `whispering campaigns' to discredit journalists who they believe are unsympathetic to their cause[59]. Rebecca Smithers, a political correspondent with the *Guardian*, claims that spindoctors make journalists feel awkward and insecure about what they write. They feel `beaten up, intellectually', as the spindoctors

---

[55] *Have they got news for you*
[56] John Sergeant interviewed in *Have they got news for you.*
[57] This was an anonymous quote attributed to Mandelson in *Have they got news for you.*
[58] Michael Brunson interviewed in *Have they got news for you*
[59] Alan Rusbridger interviewed in *Have they got news for you*

undermine the judgement of journalists and make them question the position they take[60]. John Kampfner, political correspondent with the *Financial Times*, claims that it is difficult to have open political debate in our political parties because such debate will be 'spun' as a snub to the leader of the party. MP's are becoming increasingly afraid to speak their minds, and this is leading to a lower calibre of MP[61].

Politicians have also expressed concern about the rise of spindoctors. John Underwood, of the Labour Party, claims that spindoctors contribute towards a lack of transparency in the political system. Political battles take place increasingly out of the 'public gaze', and the public thus lose faith in the system[62]. Tony Benn has taken this argument further. He does little to conceal his contempt for modern methods of political communication. Benn claims that spindoctors place stories anonymously so as to test whether they have support. If the idea proves to be unattractive, the same people repudiate it. The general public are thus deprived of reliable information. They lose confidence in politicians and refuse to believe what they read in the papers. Tony Benn claims that this undermines the democratic process. Democracy has to be open and clear. He believes that journalists should refuse to use political sources unless they are prepared to go on record and assume responsibility for their views. He claims that journalists need to unite to break the spindoctor system. If they refuse to publish stories from anonymous sources, it would force political leaders to say things themselves rather than leak stories through their spindoctors[63].

Modern democracy is increasingly about the marketing of policies, and less about fundamental philosophical differences. We live in a political culture dominated by free market ideas, and little is done to challenge this consensus in parliament and in the media. The media no longer function effectively as independent watchdogs. The political information they receive is already filtered for public consumption, and the opinions they express are often constrained by

---

[60] Rebecca Smithers interviewed in *Have they got news for you*

[61] John Kampfner interviewed in *Have they got news for you*.

[62] John Underwood interviewed in *Have they got news for you*.

[63] Tony Been interviewed in *Have they got news for you*.

the vested interests of the elite who dominate the British media. It would seem that individual journalists are funnelled by those who own the media and those who provide the media with political information.

Conclusion

The media can have an important role in the democratic process. They can monitor the economic and political system, provide us with information and facilitate debate. News which concentrates upon the personal indiscretions of MPs does not improve our understanding of the political process, nor assist us in striving for political change. Andrew Belsey has pointed out that democracy is threatened by trivialised reporting, by invasions of privacy and by distorting the truth. Democracy can only be served by journalism which is dedicated to accuracy, honesty and fairness[64]. The media can serve the democratic process, but this necessarily involves challenging those who seek to use the media to present their own particular interests as the general interest, and limit unduly the range of options open to the British public. True democracy relies upon the existence of debate, and the opportunity to participate. A media that supports such procedures would have a greater understanding of the public interest than one dedicated to pushing the establishment view. The media should assume some responsibility for the health of the democratic system. Without a vigilant media, the general public is deprived of reliable information. A media which fails to assume this responsibility protects existing inequalities in the distribution of power, and diverts attention away from real political issues. Such a media cannot make a significant contribution to the democratic system.

---

[64] A. Belsey, `Journalism and ethics: Can they co-exist ?' p10, in M. Kieran (ed), *Media Ethics*, Routledge: London, 1998, pp1-14.

3. Objectivity and bias

The idea of objectivity has become a sacred part of the journalist's vocabulary. It is used to ward off criticism of bias, and to confer legitimacy upon the profession of journalism[1]. When journalists claim that they are objective, they give the impression that they are mere conduits through which the truth is transmitted *from* the event *to* the public. Journalists are sometimes prone to deny that they have personal agendas which inform the way they report an event, and that their stories are fair, unbiased, true and written regardless of any personal views they might hold. Given these laudable qualities, the audience is urged to believe what they read, see or hear. But objectivity is an elusive concept. It gives the impression that the truth can be known in its entirety, and that reports are free from personal political preferences, selective appreciation of what is relevant, and the politics of the publisher. The idea of objectivity can be used to disguise the political agendas of the media.

The importance of objectivity and impartiality

Matthew Kieran believes that journalists should aspire to report the objective truth, and that journalism which ignores this goal can be condemned. He argues that `... it is not just illegitimate but immoral to reconstrue news events merely because a journalist's prejudices, interests or news agenda suggests things should be otherwise'[2]. He claims that good journalism is concerned with promoting our understanding of events through the use of `truth-promoting methods'. It is thus important for journalists to aim to be impartial, for partiality conceals the truth[3].

---

[1]   McNair, *News and Journalism in the UK*, p27.
[2]   M. Kieran, `Objectivity, impartiality and good journalism', p34 in M. Kieran (ed), *Media Ethics*, Routledge: London, 1998, pp23-36.
[3]   Kieran, `Objectivity, impartiality and good journalism', pp34-35.

An objective story would be one that gives all sides, that draws from a wide variety of sources, and separates facts from opinions, argument and editorial comment. Objectivity involves the presentation of facts which can be independently verified and presented without being distorted by the preferences of the presenter. It leaves out all subjective opinions about how the world should be and concentrates upon what is. An objective view of the world attempts to capture an event without bias and in total[4]. When the term objectivity is used, however, it is often inter-changeable with impartiality which involves a `... disinterested approach to news, lacking in motivation to shape or select material according to a particular view or opinion'[5]. Objectivity, by seeking to capture an event in total, would appear to be too precise for the written or spoken world. Even a picture is taken at a certain angle, and this can affect the way we interpret it. Perhaps the most we can ever expect is a `disinterested' or `unbiased' approach.

Objectivity and impartiality have not always been valued by journalists. Journalism in nineteenth century Britain was openly partisan. It represented the interests of the economic and political elite. This had to change, however, when papers sought to expand their readership. The so-called popular press included human interest and crime stories. Deference to the governing elite was not appropriate for the market, and the popular press found itself speaking for the general public and attempting to provide it with impartial knowledge[6]. Developments in technology also encouraged a move towards objective journalism. Wire services like the Associated Press in America provided news to a variety of papers, and this news had to be impartial. The development of photography and of positivist philosophical thinking also fashioned the view that it was possible to

---

[4] McNair, *News and Journalism in the UK*, p27 and p52.
[5] P. Golding and P. Elliott, `Bias, objectivity and ideology ' p412 in P. Marris and S. Thornham (eds), *Media Studies: A Reader*, Edinburgh University Press: Edinburgh, 1996, pp411-415. See also p412.
[6] Dan Schiller (1981) cited in McNair, *News and Journalism in the UK*, p28.

capture an accurate representation of the real world, independent of human values[7].

The notion that journalists should be impartial is a value associated closely with the BBC. The British Broadcasting Company was formed in 1922, and became the British Broadcasting Corporation in 1926 when it was given its royal charter. The BBC was given its charter on condition that it remained impartial. The Charter, however, also gives the Home Secretary the power to revoke the licence of the BBC. John Reith, the first Director General of the BBC, believed that it was important for the public to be educated to deliberate on public matters, and that to disregard the need to educate opinion was dangerous and stupid. He believed that the BBC existed to 'educate, entertain and inform'. It was committed to public service and aimed to enrich the intellectual, cultural and moral capabilities of the British people. It was to speak for the nation and promote social and national unity, political stability and common service in the national interest[8].

During the General Strike of 1926, Winston Churchill wanted to take over the BBC and use it as a propaganda tool against the miners. The government, however, denied him this power and argued that it was more important for the BBC to be seen as independent and impartial. John Reith argued that if the government took over the BBC during the strike, the miners would simply close it down. The general strike transformed the BBC. It became a vital news service, which included news items provided by the strikers as well as by the government. Reith wanted the BBC to interview the unions and the leadership of the Labour Party, but the Conservative government was uncomfortable with the prospect of the miners' putting their case to the nation and banned such interviews. Although the impartiality of the BBC was quite limited, the BBC emerged from the General Strike claiming that it was neutral. It had learnt to censor itself so as to avoid being censored by the government, and had come to understand that

---

[7] McNair, *News and Journalism in the UK*, pp27-29.
[8] John Reith in Eldridge, Kitzinger and Williams, *The Mass Media Power in Modern Britain*, pp45-47.

the art of effective propaganda relies not upon distorting the truth but in being selective in the presentation of information[9]. Reith believed that the BBC had to rise above politics. He believed that politics was quite sordid, and politicians insincere. Politicians were thought to be far too interested in their own popularity and power. In Reith's view, the true function of government was to administer the country in a business like and efficient manner[10]. According to the Crawford Committee, the BBC was set up as `... a cultural, moral and educative force for the improvement of knowledge, taste and manners ... a powerful means of promoting social unity'[11]. It was argued that the nation contains diverse elements, but that broadcasting should aim to nurture a common national culture. The impartiality of the BBC would always be subordinate to the `national interest'. The BBC admits that its impartiality does not necessarily mean `neutrality' on fundamental `moral and constitutional beliefs', nor does it `... feel obliged to be neutral as between truth and untruth, justice and injustice, compassion and cruelty, tolerance and intolerance'[12].

Reith's doctrines of impartiality and public service continue to dominate production values at the BBC. John Wilson, controller of editorial policy for the BBC, claimed that the BBC was established to represent the people of the country. It is a national rather than state broadcaster. Its function is to question, and this might make it seem like the BBC is attacking the fundamentals of British society[13]. Many key BBC journalists deny that the BBC is biased. Richard Sambrook rejects the view that there is a left wing trend in the BBC. Mike Byford of BBC Leeds said that the BBC has a `bias against bias', and

[9] McNair, *News and Journalism in the UK* , pp48-49, C. Ponting, *Secrecy in Britain*, Blackwell: Oxford, 1990, p35, and J. Seaton, `Broadcasting History', pp119-121 in J. Curran and J. Seaton, *Power without Responsibility*, Routledge: London, 1997, pp109-236.
[10] Seaton, `Broadcasting History', pp115-116.
[11] The Crawford Committee cited in McNair, *News and Journalism in the UK*, p30.
[12] BBC statement cited in McNair, *News and Journalism in the UK*, p31.
[13] John Wilson interviewed in *TV Images*, BBC2, 15.6.1996.

that the strength of BBC journalism is that it is accurate, fair and impartial[14]. Richard Tait of Channel 4 claims that opinion polls showed that people trust the TV news they receive from ITV and BBC far more than they trust the information they receive from newspapers. According to the film maker Ken Loach, this only shows that television has conducted a successful propaganda campaign to convince people that it is impartial and objective[15].

At first sight, an objective and impartial news service would seem to be a good thing. It could be argued that a partial news service would conceal the truth and would tend to be partisan. An impartial news service could serve democracy by expressing a variety of opinions, thereby providing reliable information necessary for public deliberation and allowing the audience to conclude for themselves. Objectivity and impartiality, however, does not necessarily expand the ideological framework within which the news is presented. The BBC, which still prides itself on being an impartial service, is usually willing to place the so-called 'national interest' above the disclosure of all information. It is generally limited in the sources it quotes and tends to favour the political establishment. Being an impartial service, albeit in a limited way, does not mean that it strays from the fundamentals of liberal democracy and capitalist economics. Alternative views of the world gain very little coverage. It would seem, indeed, that objective reporting is an unrealistic goal given the way that 'news values' are constructed, and the bias stemming from the place of the media in society.

Subjectivity and news values

The subjectivist critique of objectivity states that it is impossible for us to attain an objective version of events because we are necessarily subjective; we have a point of view, we ask certain questions which influence the answers we get, we are participants in the recording of

---

[14] Richard Sambrook and Mike Byford interviewed in *TV Images*, BBC2, 15.6.1996.
[15] Richard Tait and Ken Loach discussion in *And Finally Part One: The Metropolitan Line.*

events (or the writing of history) rather than 'neutral observers'. Objectivity can be defined as presenting things free from subjective interpretation or comment. This fails to take into account that journalists 'interpret' events[16]. Andrew Edgar argues that journalism cannot be objective because there is no 'inviolable interpretation' of an event before it is reported. The meaning of an event is determined by the way it is reported. The reporter has a role to play in the interpretation of an event and, in many ways, 'interrupts' the original activity[17]. John Keane claims that people are 'situated interpreters', and that journalists are not independent but are embedded in such things as '... the structures of the media, which set agendas, constrain the contours of possible meanings, and thereby shape what individuals think about, discuss and do from day to day'[18]. Objectivity is thus precluded by the need to interpret events and by the vested interests and particular cultures of news organisations.

The subjectivist argument is often backed by reference to such theorists as Richard Rorty. Rorty has argued that the truth is relative; it depends upon the commitments of those who are describing an event or idea. Using this line of reasoning, it would seem to be impossible for a journalist to be objective. It is pointless to condemn journalists for their handling of a particular story since all we can say is that we do not share the same view or standards. All reporting is thus recognised as being biased and contingent[19]. This view of journalism has been criticised by Kieran for reducing journalists to propagandists. Propaganda is about putting forward an interpretation of events in line with fixed social and political commitments. This, he argues, is a 'perversion of journalism proper'[20].

It is often argued that news is 'value-laden' and that journalists inevitably use their judgement when reporting an event. Kieran uses the example of a photograph taken by Crispin Rodwell for Reuters.

---

[16] A. Edgar, 'Objectivity, bias and truth', p113 in Belsey and Chadwick, *Ethical Issues in Journalism and the Media*, pp 112-129.
[17] Edgar, 'Objectivity, bias and truth', pp120-121.
[18] Keane, *The Media and Democracy*, p38.
[19] Kieran, 'Objectivity, impartiality and good journalism', pp27-28.
[20] Kieran, 'Objectivity, impartiality and good journalism', p28.

This photograph was of a young boy playing in front of a slogan painted on a wall saying 'Time for Peace'. What this photograph failed to show, however, was that the slogan read 'Time for Peace, Time to Go'. This was a republican sign, urging the British forces to leave Ireland; yet it was used, in its altered form, to symbolise a desire for peace in Ireland. Kieran seems content to acknowledge that there was no 'objective' meaning to the image, that its meaning depended upon context and '... upon how they are framed by the interpretive and evaluative commitments of those who are reporting upon it'[21]. Kieran claims that it is important to note that accepting Rodwell's photograph in this light does not mean that we understand its original intention. The photograph should be seen, rather, as a representation of '... general perceptions, hopes and fears'[22].

Values play an important role in the selection and presentation of news. Paul Willis has argued that '... once an item has been selected for transmission to the public there is already bias, some selective principle, some value, quite apart from the way it is presented'[23]. We do not receive 'all news', but that which is filtered, edited and constructed according to the interests of (and pressures exerted on) the journalist community. In many ways, the news reflects and reinforces the power of dominant interests in society. Brian McNair, for example, has argued that the news is a 'social construction' and '... a synthetic, value-laden account which carries within it the dominant assumptions and ideas of the society within which it is produced'[24]. The selection procedure takes place on a number of different levels. Some news items will be excluded, whilst others will be watered down to such a degree as to render them innocuous. Some new items will be given prominence, often to conceal or divert attention away from other stories. Walter Lippman noted as early as 1922 that there are no real objective standards in the presentation of news, for the news we receive is '... the result of a whole series of selections as to what items shall be printed, in what position they shall be printed,

---

[21] Kieran, 'Objectivity, impartiality and good journalism', p26.
[22] Kieran, 'Objectivity, impartiality and good journalism', p29.
[23] Paul Willis (1971) cited in McNair, *News and Journalism in the UK*, p32.
[24] McNair, *News and Journalism in the UK*, p33.

how much space each shall occupy, what emphasis each should have'[25].

The political left have been particularly vocal about the distorting influence of news values. Sheridan and Gardner argue that all forms of communication have social functions. There is no such thing as an impartial account, and journalists are unable to capture the world `as it is'. Instead, all reports are coloured by what is deemed to be newsworthy and interpreted according to the experiences of the reporters and editors involved, and the needs of the news organisation. Sheridan and Gardner believe that these needs `... often reflect and coincide with larger group or class interests'[26]. The political process is often portrayed as a charade, devoid of any real content and significance. Politics is reduced to personalities; all of whom are thought of as self seeking, untrustworthy, and fundamentally flawed. According to Tony Benn, the media are too preoccupied with embarrassing senior politicians. If something happens which does not cause embarrassment, it is `not news'. Benn claims that we should question what we read and see on TV, and ask ourselves who benefits from the story, who said it and why ?[27].

The film maker Ken Loach claims that TV news in Britain is subjective, partial and loaded with a political message. In a live television debate broadcast on 21 March 1995, he reviewed the TV coverage of news that day. The lead story of the day on the BBC *Six O'clock News* dealt with the resignation of Rupert Pennant-Rea, the deputy governor of the Bank of England, after his ex-mistress revealed details of their affair. Channel Four ran a story about a new policy committee being set up by the government to look into the presentation of policies. Although ITN covered a demonstration against cuts in education, it was the fifth item and featured after the Pennant-Rea resignation.

Loach believes that the running order of these stories illustrates that the media are preoccupied with snooping into the private lives of

---

[25] Lippmann cited in McNair, *An Introduction to Political Communication*, p27.
[26] Sheridan and Gardner, `Press Freedom: A Socialist Strategy', p125.
[27] Benn interviewed in *Have they got news for you.*

people, and when the news deals with politics it is primarily concerned with the presentation of policies rather than with the substance. He claims that this is in direct opposition to the nature of real debate, and that journalists and politicians are involved in a kind of ritual dance; each knowing the other's steps. The profession of journalism was said to be dominated by safe political appointees who accepted and re-enforced the interests of the establishment. They avoid any real discussion of the issues, and turn political coverage into the gossip which takes place in an exclusive club. Loach believes that journalists should concentrate more upon the core of a dispute. When dealing with the question of Europe, for example, it should ask who benefits most from the policies of the European Union rather than ask whether it will split the Conservative Party. He accuses journalists of ignoring the substance of such issues and looking instead to dramatise the rows[28].

The notion of objectivity is often used by the press and broadcasters to protect themselves from criticism. Jay Rosen, a professor of Journalism at New York University, claims that it is 'dangerous and wrongheaded' when journalists claim to be objective, free from value judgements and concerned solely with the presentation of facts. By arguing that they are objective, they imply that their critics are not. Critics of the press are often attacked for being subjective and partisan. The doctrine of objectivity allows journalists to make this claim for '... one of the most insidious effects of objectivity is that it creates a world in which journalists can live without criticism, because they are the only judges of what's objective'[29]. The doctrine of objectivity can also serve to conceal the subjective processes which take place in the selection and presentation of news. It fails to take into account that the answers we get depend upon the questions we ask, and that news is selected and presented according to what the media consider to be newsworthy.

---

[28] Ken Loach in *And Finally Part One: The Metropolitan Line*, channel 4, 21.03.1995

[29] Jay Rosen interviewed by W. Glaberson, 'Fairness, bias and judgement: Grappling with the knotty issue of objectivity in journalism', *New York Times*, 12.12.1994.

News is presented in a framework acceptable to the political culture, and in line with the agenda set by the particular media organisation. Safe political news is that which treats politics as a game rather than that which reveals the details and implications of legislation. In doing so, the media often squash real debate and help to maintain elite control of the political system.

Ideology and bias

Objectivity in journalism is retarded not only by the subjective character of news values, but also by the ideological bias which affects the presentation of news. News is ideologically biased when its presentation is informed by the political preferences of those involved in the media. This would cover everything from supporting a particular political party, to the way that certain issues are prioritised. Somebody with a right of centre bias will tend to support the interests of the capitalist class, and perhaps argue that these interests correspond to the national interest. The centre (or liberal) perspective is more likely to look at the rights of the individual and monitor the activities of the state in order to avoid corruption and guard against creeping authoritarianism. Those drawn from left of centre tend to focus upon such things as economic and social injustice, and are likely to argue that an unchecked business community will do little of its own volition to further the general good. It is unrealistic to expect a journalist to remain unaffected by all ideological approaches to economic, social and political life.

The former Conservative minister Norman Tebbitt has argued that there is bias in British broadcasting. This bias stemmed from a time when there were only a small number of channels. Bias is seen as the narrowing of view around a specific ideology. According to Tebbitt, television coverage of South Africa was motivated by a general left wing agenda. He argued that the British people were not interested in news from South Africa. Where they had the choice, they did not buy papers which dealt with this issue. In his view, South Africa was made into an issue by the broadcasting community. Tebbitt acknowledged that impartiality is difficult to achieve. It is better, therefore, to have balanced approach to programming. Television programmes should put forward a point of view, rather than aim at neutrality. He believed, however, that if the left was given a platform, so should the extreme right[30].

For writers on the left of the political spectrum, the media are thought to have a conservative bias. Herman and Chomsky argue that the American media are dominated by anti-Communist sentiments. All organisations which seem to threaten property or to advocate accommodation with the left, run the risk of being kept 'continually on the defensive'. The media are encouraged to behave in an overtly anti-Communist and reactionary way. Anti-communism is reflected in the way that former communist defectors are given the status of 'experts' on communism. It has been argued that these people display all the symptoms of those 'disappointed in love', and that their hysterical anti-communism goes unchallenged simply because it is anti-Communist. Anti-Communist campaigns have served the interests of the existing elite by squashing the American union movement, justifying the build up of arms and by supporting the persistence of economic inequalities. It is notable that the media show very little interest in atrocities committed by Americans in their fight against communism. This applies, for example, in the media's lack of coverage of American bombings in Cambodia, American support for Indonesia in its campaign against East Timor, and American support for state terrorism in Chile and Guatemala. Any serious coverage of these issues would conflict with vested interests and would be filtered out of the news[31].

The views of the British left have been put forward by such people as Ralph Miliband, Golding and Elliott, and Tony Benn. Ralph Miliband has argued that the broadcast media are only impartial in a very limited sense. The broadcast media express mainstream political views, and attempt to be fair in their dealings with the main political parties in Britain and America. Miliband argues that this '... hardly precludes a steady stream of propaganda adverse to all views which

---

[30] Norman Tebbitt interviewed in *TV Images*.
[31] Herman and Chomsky, *Manufacturing Consent* ,p33. See also pp 30-33.

fall outside the consensus. Impartiality and objectivity, in this sense, stop at the point where political consensus ends - and the more radical the dissent, the less impartial and objective the media'[32]. According to Golding and Elliott, the media mis-represent the nature of power in modern society by locating power in the political rather than the economic system. The presentation of news reflects the dominant ideology in society. It focuses upon the political management of social conflict, rather than the conflict itself. It claims to be objective and neutral, but simply draws upon the `values and beliefs of the broadest social consensus'. It presents a picture of the world which is `fundamentally unchanging', it encourages scepticism towards ideas that deviate from the dominant ideology and thus serves to block any real social change[33].

Tony Benn has been one of the most outspoken critics of media bias. He argues that British broadcasting reflects establishment views. All of the main parties share similar views on NATO, nuclear weapons, Ireland, the Middle East, trade unions, Europe and the Atlantic Alliance. Anybody who expresses views contrary to the mainstream is marginalised so as to protect the establishment. In the absence of any real divisions between the parties, the media are accused of creating `phoney debates' and of avoiding the coverage of real issues. Benn, who is famed for his hectic calendar of public meetings, claims that the British people are not interested in the petty squabbles of politicians but in such issues as education, health and employment. In his view, TV news fails to address the real problems facing humanity. He acknowledges that there is no single correct view, and that he believes that broadcasters should aim to reflect the diversity of opinion. Been feels, however, that the BBC reflects the dominant ideas of the dominant class. It was nationalised so as to ensure that the establishment had its own voice, and to convince people that there is no real alternative to the establishment view. In Benn's view, the media have assumed the role formerly held by the

---

[32] Raplph Miliband cited in McNair, *News and Journalism in the UK*, p49.
[33] Golding and Elliott, `Objectivity, Bias and Ideology', p414.

church; that of controlling people's minds in the interests of the dominant class[34].

Bias can be detected in the way that the media often lend support to those in powerful positions. Journalists give greater credence to the powerful as sources of information, and tend to marginalise the opinions and information given by the powerless. The structure and 'cultural assumptions' of the media tend to make for reports which reflect the dominant values of society rather than the perspectives which challenge these values[35]. Such bias runs counter to the principles of democracy. Theodore Glasser has argued that democracy relies upon recognising the value of the opinions of the 'ordinary citizen', and in separating the opinions expressed by people from the positions they occupy. The demands for objectivity in journalism encourages journalists to use official sources, and to report by identifying conflicting interpretations of an issue. These official interpretations are often treated as 'fact' regardless of whether they are true or valid[36].

Bias also occurs in the way that the media view parliamentary politics as the only legitimate form of political activity, and in the way they marginalise and condemn demonstrations, strikes and other forms of extra-parliamentary political action. For example, media coverage of an anti-war demonstration in London in 1968 consisted in personal attacks on the character of Tariq Ali (one of its leaders) and in presenting the demonstration as a violent clash between demonstrators and the police (even though only a few clashes occurred)[37]. Industrial disputes are often presented as the work of a Marxist-inspired minority. During the General Strike of 1926, the *Daily Mail* went so far as to say that the defeat of the strike will `...

---

[34]   Tony Benn interviewed in *And Finally Part One: The Metropolitan Line* and in *TV Images*.
[35]   Stuart Hall in McNair, *News and Journalism in the UK*, p53.
[36]   T. Glasser, 'Objectivity and News Bias', p178 in E.D. Cohen (ed), *Philosophical Issues in Journalism*, Oxford University Press: New York, 1992, pp176-185.
[37]   McNair, *News and Journalism in the UK*, p35.

end the danger of communist tyranny in Europe'[38]. The Glasgow University Media Group have pointed out that media coverage of industrial disputes during the 1970s invariably presented the workers and the unions in a bad light. The media blamed inflation upon the workers demands for higher wages, claimed that strikes had caused an economic crisis in Britain and that the workers were to blame for the strikes[39]. Media coverage of the 1984-85 miners' strike ignored the need to put forward a balanced account. The case put forward by the NUM was not covered in any depth. Siding with the government paid dividends, for sympathetic papers and news organisations gained privileged access to government ministers. A number of journalists complained about the level of bias. Nicholas Jones of BBC Radio claimed that `... stories that gave prominence to the position of the NUM could simply be omitted, shortened, or submerged into another report'[40]. Reports in the *Sunday Times* were also one sided. Journalists covering the dispute found their stories being altered, for Murdoch's papers were committed to crushing the miners in the interests of `... liberal democracy, economic recovery and the rolling back of union power'[41]. By marginalising these forms of activity, the media confer legitimacy upon the system of parliamentary democracy and the maintenance of elite rule.

There is also significant bias in the British press in favour of the Conservative Party. Lord Rothermere's papers have a declared Conservative bias. When Stewart Steven, editor of the *Mail on Sunday*, wanted to lend support to the SDP he had to get permission from Rothermere. This permission was granted because the *Mail on Sunday* target group had moved towards the SDP; once this support began to wane, the *Mail on Sunday* resumed its support for the Conservative Party[42]. The *Express* group has usually been run with a

---

[38] Curran, `Press History', p53.
[39] McNair, *News and Journalism in the UK*, pp36-37.
[40] Nicholas Jones cited in Negrine, *Politics and the Mass Media in Britain*, p66.
[41] *Sunday Times* editorial cited in Negrine, *Politics and the Mass Media in Britain*, p66.
[42] Snoddy, *The Good, the Bad and the Unacceptable*, p120.

Conservative bias, regardless of the political opinions of its readers. The *Daily Star*, for example, supported Thatcher in the 1983 General Election even though only 21% of its readers voted Conservative. The paper continued to propagate right wing views when Lord Stevens took over the *Express* Group in 1985, even though its readership tended to be dominated by those with left-of-centre views. Lord Stevens is forthright about the political bias of his newspapers. Stevens, a Tory peer, claimed that he would not want his papers to support the Labour Party because he believes that `... it is in the best interests of United Newspapers in terms of its profits and shareholders to support the Conservatives'[43].

During the 1980s, there was a clear bias in favour of the Conservative Party in much of the British press. Negrine has argued that this means that the Conservative Party `... continues to enjoy the favours of those newspaper owners who are embedded in the present structures of power and of wealth creation'[44]. At times, this bias became too absurd for the journalists on the papers. In 1983, for example, journalists on the *Daily Mail* objected to their paper's treatment of the Labour Party and demanded that it was treated in a fairer way. Negrine believes that this protest was in the `spirit of social responsibility'[45]. The case put forward by the *Mail* journalists was ultimately unsuccessful in bringing about a shift in editorial policy. It was argued by the *Mail* executive that the editor has final say in the content of the paper, and that the journalists were attempting to interfere in things that did not concern them[46]. The extent of the political bias in favour of the Conservative Party gave rise to new papers; the most notable of which is the *Independent*. The *Independent* was launched in 1986 with the declared intention of remaining free from party ties, and being fair in its treatment of all parties and ideologies. The paper has remained true to this aim and this has led one commentator to say that it is `... as if the social

---

[43] Snoddy, *The Good, the Bad and the Unacceptable*, p133.
[44] Negrine, *Politics and the Mass Media in Britain*, p55.
[45] Negrine, *Politics and the Mass Media in Britain*, p52.
[46] Negrine, *Politics and the Mass Media in Britain*, p66.

responsibility theory of the press had been translated into real newspaper practice'[47].

The British press have a reputation for being not only pro-Conservative, but also anti-Labour. This dates back to the early years of the Labour Party, and to when Ramsay MacDonald led the first minority Labour government in 1924. The Sunday tabloid *John Bull* claimed that MacDonald's birth certificate showed that he was illegitimate. *The Daily Mail* printed stories about Ramsay MacDonald using taxis and chauffeur-driven cars, and neglected to mention that MacDonald did not own his own car and that a car and chauffeur had been provided for him by a family friend for the duration of his premiership and not as a gift. By far the worst smear against MacDonald was the so-called Zinoviev Letter. During the General Election Campaign of 1924, the *Daily Mail* published a story which stated that Grigori Zinoviev (the president of the Communist International) had written a letter to the British Communist Party stating that Ramsay MacDonald's Labour government was involved in a Bolshevik plot to thrust Britain into a civil war and paralyse its defences. Although it was suspected that this letter was a forgery, the *Daily Mail* declared that it was `duty bound' to publish it. It was revealed in the 1960s that the letter had been written by Russian exiles in Berlin. This campaign against the Labour Party also involved the *Daily Mirror* which urged its readers to `Vote British, not Bolshie'. This smear paid high political dividends. Although the Labour Party increased its share of the vote (because of the continued decline of the Liberal Party), the hysteria created by the press is thought to have increased the turn-out at the election, increased support for the Conservative Party and contributed to the Conservative electoral victory[48].

Although these tactics might seem primitive and ludicrous, acidic coverage of the Labour Party has continued to play a role in British politics into the 1990s. Lord Wakeham, a former Conservative minister, admitted that the press had a decisive role in securing the

---

[47] Negrine, *Politics and the Mass Media in Britain*, p51.
[48] Snoddy, *The Good, the Bad and the Unacceptable*, pp26-28, and Curran, `Press History', p52.

defeat of Labour in the General Election of 1992. He claimed that `...
the sharpness of the pro-Conservative newspapers' comments and the
depth and breadth of their reporting undoubtedly helped to ensure
some of the movement towards us in the last weeks of the
campaign'[49]. The press was particularly important in undermining
Labour with the *Daily Mail* coverage of Labour's `tax bombshell',
the *Sunday Times* story on `Kinnock and the Kremlin Connection',
and the *Sun* headline `If Kinnock wins today, will the last person to
leave Britain turn out the lights'[50]. Lord McAlpine, a key fund raiser
for the Conservative Party, said that the press had mounted a
`comprehensive' attack on the Labour Party and had `... exposed,
ridiculed and humiliated the party, doing each day in their pages the
job that the politicians failed to do from their bright new platforms'[51].

The extent of anti-Labour bias in the British press has created
serious problems for the Labour Party. Roy Hattersley claims that it
is impossible to win elections without the support of the tabloids.
This has meant that New Labour has been careful not to alienate the
tabloids in general, and Rupert Murdoch in particular[52]. During the
early 1970s, Murdoch's paper the *Sun* was critical of the Conservative
government of Edward Heath and supported the miners strike of
1973-1974. By 1979, however, the paper had swung to the right and
gave its full support to Mrs Thatcher. On election day in 1979 it
called for *Sun* readers to vote Conservative to `stop the rot'. Larry
Lamb, the editor of the *Sun*, was thanked for his support and given a
knighthood for his services to journalism[53]. Rupert Murdoch
remained loyal to the Thatcher government throughout the 1980s.
Thatcher's advocacy of the free market was in accordance with

---

[49] Lord Wakeham cited in McNair, `Journalism, politics and public relations', p57.
[50] McNair, `Journalism, politics and public relations', p57, and Eldridge, Kitzinger and Williams, *The Mass Media Power in Modern Britain*, p40.
[51] Lord McAlpine cited in McNair, `Journalism, politics and public relations', pp57-58.
[52] Roy Hattersley interviewed in *Blair's Year*.
[53] Eldridge, Kitzinger and Williams, *The Mass Media Power in Modern Britain*, pp33-34.

Murdoch's views and business interests. It was not until the mid-1990s that the Murdoch group turned against the Conservative government. It has been argued that Murdoch's switch to New Labour was motivated by commercial considerations. Recognising that New Labour could win the next election, Murdoch turned against the Conservatives and seemed to offer his support in return for favourable regulations on the ownership and control of the media[54].

There is widespread bias in the British and American media. This bias helps to legitimise and protect inequalities in the economic system. Political parties that have dedicated themselves to alleviating (or abolishing) these inequalities have found it difficult to get a fair hearing in the media. The media have had a devastating effect upon left of centre politics in Britain and America. They tend to support the existing system and use their power to marginalise radical dissent. In some cases, this has been expressed in Britain in terms of a clear bias in favour of the Conservative Party. The Labour Party has responded by trying to make itself more appealing to the media. This has meant abandoning many of its overtly socialist aims. Ideological bias does, however, go far beyond mere party preference. Jay Rosen has argued that ideological bias in less worrying that the bias enshrined in the 'conventions of journalism'. Bias is apparent and expressed in the way that journalists set the framework for political debate, and in the way they emphasise the '... winning and the game of politics'[55]. By trivialising political coverage, the media divert attention away from core issues. We are sometimes left knowing more about the personal lives of politicians, than about the long term goals of the government.

Conclusion

The pursuit of objectivity does not necessarily produce the best form of journalism. The notion of objectivity encourages journalists to be impartial, yet can result in retarding their critical faculties. The

---

[54] Eldridge, Kitzinger and Williams, *The Mass Media Power in Modern Britain*, p41.
[55] Rosen interviewed by Glaberson, 'Fairness, bias and judgement'.

objective journalist is meant to be a dis-interested spectator, rather than somebody who should aspire to originality in thinking. Research on the American press shows that a considerable number of Washington correspondents consider themselves incapable of understanding the political processes and policies upon which they are reporting[56]. The idea of objectivity can also serve to undermine the social responsibilities of the media. By arguing that news exists independently of the reporter, the reporter is able to deny any responsibility for what is reported. The idea of objectivity allows the reporter to claim that the news is 'fact', rather than something created by the journalist. Glasser argues, indeed, that '... journalists today are largely amoral. Objectivity in journalism effectively erodes the very foundation on which rests a responsible press'[57]. By arguing that objective reporting is possible because the news exists independently of the reporter, the journalist not only avoids responsibility for what is reported but also accountability for the consequences of a news report. Walter Cronkite, indeed, believed that reporters should simply report and ignore the moral, political, social and economic consequences of what is reported[58]. Glasser claims that we will not have a responsible press until journalists are held accountable for the consequences of their reports. Journalists are responsible for the news because the news is created by them. Journalists will often resist this line of argument and use the doctrine of objectivity to protect themselves. Objectivity is not a pure standard to which all reporters must aspire. It is a custom and habit of mind which serves the interests of the owners of the press far more than it serves the needs of society[59].

---

[56] Cohen, *Philosophical Issues in Journalism*, pp158-159, and Glasser, 'Objectivity and News Bias', p176.
[57] Glasser, 'Objectivity and News Bias', p176.
[58] Glasser, 'Objectivity and News Bias', p183.
[59] Glasser, 'Objectivity and News Bias', p183.

4. The Public and the Private

The arguments for freedom of speech and freedom of the press were developed originally to increase public debate and widen access to political information. These freedoms are important so that we know what our representatives are doing on our behalf, and to safeguard against the state increasing its power to the detriment of the public. Yet the public has become increasingly interested in the private lives of public figures. Ellen Goodman, a political columnist with the *Boston Globe*, has noted how the American press justifies its intrusion into the personal lives of politicians on the grounds that we can gain greater understanding of where these politicians are leading the country. She noted that the press used to be far more restrained. For example, it never showed President Franklin Roosevelt getting in and out of his wheelchair, nor did it pay any attention to the sexual antics of President Kennedy. She doubts whether details about the distinctive features of President Clinton's genitals can tell the public a great deal about his public administration[1]. The division between the public and the private is becoming increasingly blurred, and this has created a recurring problem for the media, their audience and their victims.

The importance of privacy

The right to privacy is often regarded as a fundamental feature of liberal democracies. It effectively draws a line between the individual and society and makes it known that there is and must be a limit to the jurisdiction of the state and other people in the affairs of the individual. The nature and social implications of the right to privacy are, however, far from straight forward. We may wish to grant ourselves the right to privacy, but what we include in this category will not necessarily correspond with the priorities valued by other

---

[1] Ellen Goodman, `Pacific Coast Center Political Briefing Breakfast number 3', http:www.freedomforum.org/freedomforum/oakland/break3elleng.html

people. In a world of isolated individuals, privacy would be a relatively simple matter. Our personal and professional obligations toward other people, however, mean that the degree of privacy we have as individuals is of social concern.

Early definitions of privacy, such as the one put forward by Cooley in 1888, defined it as the 'right to be let alone'[2]. Such a broad definition of privacy is, however, of limited value. The Younger Report of 1972 claimed that '... such a formula turns out on closer examination, to go so far beyond any right which the individual living in an organised society could reasonably claim, that it would be useless as a basis for the granting of legal protection'[3]. Privacy is not just the absence of something, but the right to such things as consideration and respect. A.F. Westin described it in terms of our desire to determine for ourselves how much personal information is communicated to others. It amounts to a '...voluntary and temporary withdrawal of a person from the general society'[4]. If we claim a right to privacy, we are attempting to defend ourselves against public scrutiny. The definition of public can mean those closest to us as well as the multitudes reached by contemporary media. We are saying, in effect, that as individuals there is and must be a domain which is special to ourselves and is of no concern to anybody else. If this domain is intruded upon, we may wish to claim that our moral (if not legal) rights have been infringed.

Westin has outlined four basic states of privacy which he defines as solitude, intimacy, anonymity and reserve. Solitude is where we are free from group relations and group observation, and are thus free to explore our own minds and conscience. Intimacy is where solitude is broken in exchange for close relations with another person (a partner, for example) or with a small group. The third type of privacy is anonymity. This is where we are in public but seek freedom from surveillance. Finally, there is reserve where we hold back information about ourselves and create a 'mental distance' which can protect our

---

[2] Cooley cited in I.N. Stevens and D.C.M. Yardley, *The Protection of Liberty*, Blackwell: Oxford, 1982, pp159-160.

[3] The Younger Report cited in Yardley, *The Protection of* Liberty, p160.

[4] A.F. Westin, *Privacy and Freedom*, Bodley Head: London, 1967, p7.

personalities[5]. What unites these four states of privacy is that they view the individual as being potentially under threat from the wider public. They see privacy from the point of view of the individual and imply that we need protection from the scrutiny and surveillance of others. They do not, however, suggest what we can do if our privacy has been compromised. These forms of privacy (with the possible exception of intimacy), can be described as `negative'. They are, indeed, refinements of the `right to be let alone' view of privacy.

 Privacy also has `positive' aspects, for it relies upon the co-operation of other people and of the state. Without this co-operation, we would not have the conditions necessary for us to enjoy our privacy. It could also be argued that we should have access to information held on us by the institutions of the state. Whilst we are denied this information, our privacy is infringed. We need to be sure, moreover, that the procedures for intruding upon other people's privacy are known and are observed[6]. These `positive' aspects of privacy concentrate upon the motives and activities of those who intrude or who have the power to intrude upon our privacy. Instead of simply claiming that we must have the right to privacy, the positive aspects show that we must seek to control the activities of those who would intrude upon our privacy or, at the very least, make these individuals and organisations accountable for their actions. Privacy, viewed in this way, is not so much the absence of scrutiny and surveillance but active control over our own lives and over the surveillance procedures of society.

 The desire for privacy is, in some ways, a product of the modern age. The development of so called `mass society' makes privacy a precious commodity. Technological changes have made it easier for others to intrude and to communicate their findings to an ever increasing audience. Against this, we might feel deprived of privacy; both in terms of not being left alone and in terms of lacking control over those who would intrude. The desire for privacy is not a universal nor static phenomenon. It has not been valued by all

[5] Westin, *Privacy and Freedom*, pp31-32.
[6] Feldman, *Civil Liberties and Human Rights in England and Wales*, p357.

cultures, at all times and in all circumstances. It is, to a far greater degree, something we value when we feel that our rights have been infringed. In order to feel this, there must be an underlying belief that we have a right to privacy and that it is of individual and social value. Such beliefs have not always been prevalent.

In ancient times, the private sphere was seen as inferior to the public sphere. Indeed, whoever was confined solely to the private sphere was regarded as in some way not fully human. The private sphere catered for the `necessities of life'. Although the ancient Greeks drew a sharp distinction between the two spheres (to the detriment of the private), the ancient Romans saw that the private sphere offered a temporary refuge from the demands of the public sphere. Here lies, according to Hannah Arendt, the origins of modern privacy[7]. The example of ancient society illustrates how privacy and social responsibility can be seen to exist in an antagonistic relationship. Service to the Greek polis made private life and privacy a secondary concern. Even in Roman times, it was not that privacy was valued for its own sake; but for allowing the individual to re-charge before entering the public arena once more. The obligations of citizenship pervaded the ancient world. They set the criteria against which the individual was judged.

The medieval world changed the criteria from serving the state to serving God. With this change, privacy attained increased significance. Christian mysticism encouraged individual contemplation and solitude from other humans. In this way, the individual was able to communicate with God. Walter Hilton, for example, discusses the importance of people living contemplative and devout lives. Only in this way can they attain `spiritual perfection'. In order to achieve this, the individual (man in Hilton's case) must `... enter into himself and come to the knowledge of his own soul ... (he) must withdraw his mind from love of all earthly creatures, from vain thoughts, and images of all sensible things, and from all self-love'[8]. Privacy, or withdrawal from the public world, was thus necessary to

---

[7] See Hannah Arendt in S. Lukes, *Individualism*, Blackwell: Oxford, 1973, p60.
[8] Hilton cited in Lukes, *Individualism*, p61.

communicate with God. The Renaissance, however, shifted the priorities once again. The Renaissance, by undermining the power of the Church, made privacy an end in itself or, as Berlin called it, something `... sacred in its own right'[9].

These changes show that the value of privacy depends upon the weight we confer upon things outside of the individual. If we claim that the polis is more important than the individual, then privacy is relatively unimportant. Serving the polis or society involves `outward' or `public' acts. Privacy can thus detract from the greater good. Serving God (at least for the Medievals) entailed greater introspection. The individual was still in a subordinate position (this time to God and to the Church), but required the space to meditate and communicate with the deity.

Privacy becomes increasingly important to the extent that we value individuals for who they are, rather than for what they serve. This is reflected, with a reasonable amount of clarity, in liberal social theory. It was clearly Mill's intention to defend the individual from unwanted and unwarranted interference by other people. Mill wanted to preserve a space for the individual to grow; unfettered by the opinions and intrusion of others. He believed that the individual's need for privacy meant that there were circumstances in which the `truth' should be suppressed. These circumstances were when `... the truth, without being of any advantage to the public, is calculated to give annoyance to private individuals'[10]. These circumstances were described by Mill as the `... one case, and only one, in which there might appear to be some doubt of the propriety of permitting the truth to be told without reserve'[11]. Liberals believe that we need privacy in self-regarding matters.

Privacy can be seen as indispensable to democracy because it shields individuals and groups from public intrusion. Most democracies have respect for family life, and show tolerance towards

---

[9] Berlin cited in Lukes, *Individualism*, p62.
[10] J.S. Mill, `Law of Libel and Liberty of the Press' (1825) pp160-161, in G.L. Williams (ed), *John Stuart Mill on Politics and Society*, Fontana: 1976, pp143-169.
[11] Westin, *Privacy and Freedom*, p26.

such things as religious diversity and group membership. This helps to protect our privacy. Privacy, however, can also pose a threat to democracy. By concentrating upon private matters, we might become indifferent to our rights and/or obligations as citizens. Privacy amongst organisations might conceal the influence they have over public policy, and can be used to frustrate our right to know and hide abuses in power[12]. Edward Shils believes that the aim of liberal democracy should be to create a state of political `civility' where there is enough privacy for the individual to grow and for members of the government to make policy, but where there is also enough `publicity' to keep the public politically informed[13]. In the privacy debate, therefore, we are often faced with a trade off between the rights of the individual to enjoy a `personal' life, and our need to place restraints upon those in power.

Andrew Belsey claims that we have no real right to privacy and that at least some private information should be in the public domain. In criticising the notion of privacy, he looks at the self, the community and the group. He claims that it is wrong to defend privacy by emphasising the importance of the self because this can lead to isolating the self from broader influences. The self, as Sandra Marshall has pointed out, is a `social creation' and our sense of self is gained through our relations with others. Our sense of self relies upon other people respecting that we are individuals with our own beliefs, and giving us this respect without knowing our beliefs[14]. The self is not isolated, but part of a broader community. Belsey claims that `... life is a synchronic balance between the outwardness of living in society and that inner retreat we call privacy'[15]. In his view, there needs to be a healthy balance between the self and the community. He believes that it is important to find a resting place between the extremes of the recluse and the exhibitionist; both extremes were

---

[12] Westin, *Privacy and* Freedom, pp24-25.

[13] Shils in Westin, *Privacy and* Freedom, p26.

[14] A. Belsey, `Privacy, Publicity and Politics', pp81-82 in A. Belsey and R. Chadwick (eds), *Ethical Issues in Journalism and the Media*, Routledge: London, 1992, pp72-92.

[15] Belsey, `Privacy, Publicity and Politics', p82.

referred to as 'pathological'[16]. It is also important to recognise that we share privacy with other individuals. Institutions do not have the right to privacy. It is thus an abuse of power for institutions to side-track investigations into their operations by claiming that it involves a violation of their privacy[17].

The right to privacy is recognised by the European Convention on Human Rights. Article 8 of the Convention states that everyone has '... the right to respect of his private and family life, his home and his correspondence'[18]. Public authorities, however, maintain the right to intervene in the interests of national security, public safety, the economic well being of the country, to prevent crime, to protect morals and health, or to promote the 'rights and freedoms of others'. Article 10 grants the right to freedom of expression. Once again, however, this can be restricted in the interests of national security, public safety, health and morality, to prevent crime, to protect individual reputation, to protect information received in confidence and to maintain the 'impartiality of the judiciary'[19]. Although there are plans to incorporate the European convention, British law at present does not recognise a distinct right to privacy. Individual privacy is protected by laws relating to trespass (which prevents physical intrusion on land or property, but does not apply to spying at a distance) breach of confidence and electronic bugging without permission of the property owner. There remains, however, plenty of room for the media to intrude. British journalists can effectively publish anything they wish to about a person, as long as it is not defamatory. This freedom can obviously be exploited.

It is important that individuals have some right to privacy. The mental well being of most of us relies upon having at least some time away from the scrutiny of others. If we stop demanding our right to privacy, the state and other public bodies would be given even greater

[16] Belsey, 'Privacy, Publicity and Politics', p82.
[17] Belsey, 'Privacy, Publicity and Politics', pp82-83.
[18] European Convention on Human Rights cited in M. Cloonan, 'The Press Part One: Philosophical Issues: Free Speech and the Right to Privacy', *Case Studies for Politics 10*, University of York, p13.
[19] Cloonan, 'The Press Part One', p13.

scope to intrude into the private realm. In modern times, we have become accustomed to view privacy as an end in itself. This is not necessarily good for society. It is important that we recognise our social responsibilities as well as defend our rights as individuals. We are social creations, and the lives we lead do have an effect upon others. Claiming that we should have a right to privacy should not be taken to mean that those in public life be allowed to conceal information about their public duties. It is important that we know about the public functions of an individual, whilst leaving the individual enough privacy and room to grow. Drawing a line between the public and the private is rarely straight forward. The media have found it particularly difficult to apply this distinction when dealing with politicians and royalty.

Politicians and privacy

Some regard media intrusion into the lives of politicians as being in the interests of democracy. Stuart Hall, for example, claims that `... everyone now knows what was once privileged information for the political class and a few others'[20]. Martin Jacques adds to this by claiming that we are witnessing a significant cultural change in society. Intimate details of a politician's sexual behaviour `... would have once been treated with disgust, now it is read with relish'[21]. Knowing something intimate about those in power may well help to close the gap between representatives and the represented, but this does not necessarily mean that it serves democracy. A vibrant democratic system relies upon the existence of informed debate. Access to salacious details about those in power might discourage an interest in politics, and justify mass apathy, on the basis that power corrupts.

Martin Jacques has argued that media preoccupation with `the personal' runs the risk of trivialising politics. This can be seen in America where policy is covered in a decreasing amount of depth. He

---

[20]   Stuart Hall cited in M. Jacques, `The New Democracy', *The Observer*, 8.12.1998.
[21]   Jacques, `The New Democracy'

claims, however, that it would be wrong to ignore the contribution that this form of reporting makes to democracy, for sex and intimate details offer `... a universal language in a way that traditional politics rarely did'[22]. In his view, democracy has entered a new era: the `era of the personal'[23]. It could be argued that the personalising of politics has made it accessible and interesting to a wider range of people. A dry policy document on the use of drugs, for example, can become far more interesting if it is revealed that those framing the legislation have personal experience of drug use. It could lead many to ask if there was one law for those in power, and another for the rest of us. This question could contribute towards a demand for greater democracy and more access to information.

The circulation of the tabloids in Britain illustrate that people are interested in the `private' over the `public'. This has been explained in a number of ways. The psychologist Oliver James has argued that British people have become obsessed with how they compare with others. Whereas we used to venerate celebrities, this is no longer the case. We continue to admire those in the public eye, but yearn to see their downfall[24]. Joyce Macmillan explains our collective interest in the private lives of public figures in terms of a change in the nature of power. She argues that we have moved away from the traditional patriarchal conception of politics which concentrated upon nation states, military conflict and espionage. This was a `big boys' game and had little or no room for personal concerns. People are increasingly aware, however, that politicians have relatively little power and that the most important decisions are made by the business community[25]. Martin Jacques continues this line of argument and claims that our pre-occupation with the personal can be traced to the re-emergence of feminism in the 1960s, which taught us that power resides not only in the government, but in many areas of public and

---

[22] Jacques, `The New Democracy'.
[23] Jacques, `The New Democracy'.
[24] Oliver James in Jacques, `The New Democracy'.
[25] Joyce Macmillan in Jacques, `The New Democracy'.

private life. Our view of what is political was thus broadened to include the personal[26].

It has been suggested that the public should be informed about `... private behaviour which affects or may affect the conduct of public business'[27]. This seems to apply, in particular, to instances of hypocrisy. In July 1992, for example, The *Independent* newspaper published revelations that Virginia Bottomley (Minister of Health) had been an unmarried teenage mother. This story was published during a government campaign against teenage pregnancies. The publication of details concerning the affair of David Mellor (Heritage Minister) with Antonia da Sancha was also justified in the `public interest'. The *People* newspaper bugged Ms. Da Sancha's rented flat. This was done with the permission of her landlord. The *People* argued that the story was in the public interest because Mellor was heard to say that the affair was leaving him `seriously knackered', and that this affected his ability to write ministerial speeches   A broader justification for publishing this story is that Mr. Mellor and Ms. Bottomley were part of a government concerned with promoting family values[28]. Embarking upon such moral crusades left them vulnerable.

Many commentators in the field of media ethics have argued that politicians do not deserve to be shielded from media intrusion. Andrew Belsey believes that sex scandals involving politicians should not be concealed in the name of privacy. He believes that those in public life must be open to public scrutiny. This is the only way to avoid corruption in public life and it is consistent with democracy that `... those who wield power cannot decide for themselves where to draw the boundary between the public and the private aspects of their lives'[29]. Whilst the `genuinely personal' aspects of a politicians life

---

[26] Jacques, `The New Democracy'.
[27] Calcutt Report cited in Cloonan, `The Press Part One: Philosophical Issues: Free Speech and the Right to Privacy', p8.
[28] Cloonan, `The press part One', pp9-10 and M. Cloonan, `The Press Part Two: Invading Privacy: Three Cases From Modern Britain', *Case Studies for Politics 11*, University of York, p3.
[29] Belsey, `Privacy, Publicity and Politics', p78.

should be protected from public scrutiny, it should be recognised that the range of what is 'personal' is smaller and less secure in the case of politicians[30]. Politicians should not have their personal lives protected if they fall foul of the values they advocate. Belsey does not favour sensationalist coverage of sex scandals. Instead, he believes that society needs a more healthy (and tolerant) attitude towards sexual relations. This would lessen the need to be hypocritical about such things. He believes that the media have an 'ethical responsibility' to '... fight bigotry and hypocrisy and to promote a new enlightened atmosphere about sex'[31].

David Archard has identified four common justifications for media intrusion into the sexual indiscretions of politicians. The first (the 'Victorian view') is that private immorality disqualifies a person from public office. To hold public office, a person must be of untarnished character. This is considered unrealistic. The second justification is that the adulterer is a hypocrite; though simply because somebody cheats in marriage, there is no reason to believe that he or she is a hypocrite in all matters. The third justification is that somebody who cheats in marriage, will also cheat in public life. This was levelled at David Mellor by his estranged father-in law. There is no reason to believe, however, that an adulterer will be any less reliable in public life. The fourth justification states that affairs distract a minister from his or her duties. Archard argues that this justification of press intrusion '... has the desperate air of self-serving rationalisation'[32].

Archard believes, however, that media intrusion can be justified in terms of the 'interests of the public'. An intrusive media often appeal to interests of the public, but find it difficult to justify their actions in the public interest. Archard rejects the rigid distinction between the 'public interest' and the 'interests of the public'. He claims that society can benefit from knowing about the private affairs of public figures, and that gossip can have a socially useful function. It can, in

---

[30] Belsey, 'Privacy, Publicity and Politics', pp85-86.

[31] Belsey, 'Privacy, Publicity and Politics' p89.

[32] D. Archard, 'Privacy, the public interest and a prurient public', p90 in M. Kieran (ed), *Media Ethics*, Routledge: London, 1998, pp82-96. See also pp89-90.

particular, help to define and maintain social groups and serve to include or exclude people from these groups. Gossip also provides a way for groups and the community to test their moral beliefs, and by shaming those who deviate from these values, it can act as a deterrent to others. It helps to 'de-mystify' the pretentious and reduce them to a more mundane level. By exposing the private lives of public characters, we gain a far greater understanding of these people than if we concentrated solely upon their public persona[33].

The private lives of politicians are often regarded as a legitimate area of concern by those involved in the production and consumption of news. It is almost as if by entering public life, politicians make a pact with the public to be honest and conscientious in all public matters, and to apply the same principles to their private lives. Politicians, however, are rather less concerned with the private lives of individuals than with economic, social and defence policy. The modern state can certainly intrude into the private realm, but it is not the case that politicians and the public have entered into an explicit arrangement in which they judge each other on equal terms on all matters regarding personal conduct. We might want to defend media scrutiny of politicians on the grounds that it can help to combat corruption in public life. It is questionable, however, whether detailed media coverage of sexual misconduct does anything significant to assist or nurture democratic life.

Privacy and Royalty: The death of a princess

The death of Princess Diana in August 1997 prompted extreme anger towards the British media and led many to question again the relationship between the public and the private. Royalty is an archaic institution based upon hereditary power; the existence of which detracts from democracy in Britain. The royal family does not stand for election, and it's powers are inherited, mysterious and far-reaching. Its presence also helps to establish and reinforce a class system based upon breeding and inherited wealth. All of these

---

[33] Archard, 'Privacy, the public interest and the prurient public', pp90-92.

arguments (and many more) could be used against the existence of royalty, but they neither explain nor justify media preoccupation with the private lives of the royal family. Whereas politicians choose to enter public life (perhaps for a limited time), many members of the royal family seem to have rather less choice over the way they spend their lives. Many have found it virtually impossible to hold onto some remnants of a private life.

The private world of Princess Diana was particularly prone to media intrusion. She became a fashion icon and one of most glamorous symbols of the 1980s. In the 1990s, however, she found life in the royal family and the constant media attention difficult to bear. As her marriage began to collapse, the press and the public became ever more fascinated. The process began in 1992, when the *Sunday Times* serialised Andrew Morton's intimate biography *Diana: Her True Story*. This book revealed that Diana suffered from an eating disorder and that Prince Charles had had an affair with Camilla Parker-Bowles. Andrew Morton had interviewed some of Diana's closest friends, and had the full support and participation of Princess Diana for the book. This co-operation was kept secret, leaving Morton to take any flak arising from the publication. Andrew Neil justified the serialisation of Morton's book in the *Sunday Times* on the grounds that Princess Diana wanted the public to know her side of the story, that the public had a right to know things of constitutional significance and that the coverage was preferable to the secrecy that had surrounded the private life and eventual abdication of King Edward in 1936[34].

Morton and the *Sunday Times* were condemned by some sections of the British press. Max Hastings of the *Telegraph* said that the Murdoch group was guilty of publishing rubbish, and he questioned Murdoch's intentions. Hastings believed that the Morton revelations were un-true and that (even if they were true) such things should not be made public. In retrospect, Hastings admitted that responsible

---

[34]   McNair, `Journalism, politics and public relations', p59, and *Royals and Reptiles: Part 4*, Channel Four, 9.11.1997

journalists should not hold such views, and that Princess Diana's use of the Murdoch press had been both foolish and self-destructive[35].

The Morton serialisation was also condemned by the Press Complaints Commission (PCC). When Buckingham Palace denied that Diana had co-operated in the project, Lord McGregor of the PCC described the Morton book as an intrusive and `... odious exhibition of journalists dabbling their fingers in other people's souls'[36]. The PCC had to back down, however, when Princess Diana gave indirect support to the Morton book. The tabloids were tipped off that she would be visiting Caroline Bartholomew, who had provided Morton with information This was interpreted as Diana's way of giving her approval, and led Lord McGregor to conclude that she had invaded her own privacy[37].

Princess Diana's involvement in the Morton book created widescale media speculation about the future of the royal marriage, and about Diana's next move. In July 1992, it was revealed in the *Spectator* that Rupert Murdoch's paper the *Sun* had possession of some tapes which could harm the royals. These tapes were of conversations between James Gilbey and Princess Diana, in which she complained about the way she was being treated by the royal family. The tapes had been illegally recorded by a radio ham who had intercepted the signal from their mobile phones. The tapes had not been published because the media in general and the *Sun* in particular feared the imposition of a privacy law. In August 1992, however, the *National Enquirer* published a transcript of the tapes, and extracts appeared in the *Express*. As this material was now in the public domain, the *Sun* went ahead and published the tapes under the title of `Dianagate'. The *Sun* justified the publication of this material by claiming that it followed on from Diana's own involvement in the Morton book. Diana had opened a `can of worms', and now had to face the consequences[38].

---

[35] Max Hastings interviewed in *Royals and Reptiles: Part 4*

[36] Lord McGregor statement to the press in *Royals and Reptiles: Part 4.*

[37] *Royals and Reptiles: Part 4.*

[38] *Royals and Reptiles: Part 4*

When Prince Charles and Princess Diana announced their separation, the media continued to play a role in the dismantling of the marriage. Princess Diana blamed Camilla Parker-Bowles for their separation. This led the media to scrutinise Parker-Bowles and the publication of the 'Camilla Tapes'. These tapes, consisting of conversations between Prince Charles and Camilla Parker-Bowles, were published in an Australian magazine owned by Rupert Murdoch. Prince Charles responded by using the media to put across his side of the story. He was interviewed by Jonathan Dimbleby for a special documentary. Dimbleby was instructed by Prince Charles that nothing was to be done to harm the reputation of Diana, and in the interview he admitted to having an affair with Mrs. Parker Bowles. Many of the tabloids were outraged. According to Jonathan Dimbleby, the tabloids were envious because his documentary meant that they could no longer speculate on the relationship between Charles and Mrs. Parker Bowles[39].

In response to intense media intrusion, Princess Diana decided to reduce her public role. She claimed that she wanted to lead a more private life, and called for the media to respect her privacy. What this created, however, was a world-wide market for pictures and stories of her 'off duty'. The media, fearing political repercussions, employed free-lance paparazzi to trail Diana wherever she went. It was during this period that the grossest invasions of privacy occurred. In November 1993, for example, the *Mirror* Group Newspapers published photographs of Princess Diana exercising in a private gym. These photographs were taken by a concealed camera. *The Mirror* justified their publication by claiming that they were in the public interest. It claimed that the photographs had not been taken by its own photographers, and that the incident showed the potential security-risk for the Princess of Wales[40]. Lord McGregor of the PCC was incensed by the activities of the *Mirror*, and accused it of '... deliberately breaching the ethical boundaries which mark out an

---

[39] Jonathan Dimbleby interviewed in *Royals and Reptiles: Part 4*

[40] Cloonan, 'The Press Part One', p10 and B. Franklin and R. Pilling, 'Market, moguls and media regulation' p116, in M. Kieran (ed), *Media Ethics*, Routledge: London, 1998, pp111-122.

agreed competitive playing field for newspapers'[41]. The incident exposed, however, a serious weakness in the PCC. The *Mirror* retaliated by withdrawing (albeit temporarily) from the PCC, and threatening to deprive the PCC of its £100,000 a year contribution and scuttling prospects for the effective self-regulation of the press. Interventions by other papers encouraged the *Mirror* to re-join the PCC and re-commit to the principles of self-regulation[42].

Princess Diana sought to create an alliance with some sections of the media. She used the media to publicise her own charity work, and co-operated with journalists at the *Daily Mail* so as to ensure that her views on the royal family were made public. The royal family claimed that Princess Diana was mad, and attempted to discredit her. Princess Diana argued that the royal family were guilty of a `dirty tricks' campaign. She also told Richard Kaye at the *Mail* that media intrusion into her private life were akin to rape. This led to further criticisms by the royal family. Finally, Princess Diana went on record and appeared on a special edition of *Panorama*. In this programme, she discussed the problems that she had with the royal family, the relationship between Charles and Camilla Parker-Bowles, and admitted to her own affair with James Hewitt. This merely fuelled media interest in her private life[43].

In August 1997, Princess Diana was killed in a car crash. The media had become fascinated with her relationship with Dodi Al Fayed. The *Sunday Mirror* had published photographs of them kissing in France, and the media followed them for the rest of their vacation. She was killed, fleeing from the paparazzi; some of whom took pictures of her dying. Ann Leslie of the *Daily Mail* claims that there were three sides to the royal marriage. It amounted to an `almost abusive relationship' between Diana, the public and the paparazzi. Princess Diana was partly responsible for this. She had made a `pact with the devil'. She wanted public approval, just as the

---

[41]   Lord McGregor cited in Franklin and Pilling, `Market, moguls and media regulation', p116.
[42]   Franklin and Pilling, `Market, moguls and media regulation', p116, and *Royals and Reptiles : Part 4*
[43]   *Royals and Reptiles: Part 4*

public wanted to know about her. According to Leslie, Princess Diana was like a force of nature. She behaved like a dangerous, unstable meteor or `unguided missile'. It was therefore unrealistic for her to refuse to be photographed. The public also shared responsibility. Leslie claims that the public created a market for these photographs by buying the papers carrying pictures of Diana. The public might want to blame the newspapers for the death of Diana, but this is blatant hypocrisy. Leslie believes that the solution is not to be found in the introduction of a privacy law, but in members of the public changing what they want[44]. This defence places a barrier between the media and the public. It absolves the media from any direct responsibility for the death of Princess Diana, and repeats the view that the media merely respond to the demands and tastes of the public.

Many members of the press feel that Princess Diana had manipulated them and had developed a strange and inconsistent siege mentality which had regrettably back-fired. Piers Morgan, editor of the *Mirror*, has noted that the royals are `... happy to dance with the devil when it suits them'[45]. Max Hastings of the *Telegraph* claimed that Princess Diana had a `schizophrenic attitude towards stardom and towards being photographed', and believed that she would have been unhappy if she had been left alone. According to Hastings, without media attention she would have `withered on the vine'[46]. The British public, however, seem less forgiving. Two months after the death of Princess Diana, an ICM poll for the *Guardian* found that 81% of respondents believed that the royal family should be protected by a privacy law, but only 55% believed that celebrities deserved this protection, and only 45% would extend it to include politicians[47].

Media intrusion into the private life of Princess Diana is often justified by claiming that she and Prince Charles invaded their own privacy by providing the media with information and by taking part in

---

[44] Ann Leslie, interviewed by Peter Sissons on *BBC News*,
[45] Piers Morgan cited in H. Searls, `The Rights and Wrongs of Privacy' p18, *LM*, October 1997, pp15-19.
[46] Max Hastings interviewed in *Royals and Reptiles: Part 4.*
[47] Petley, `The Regulation of Media Content', p143.

lengthy television interviews. Some members of the media are prone to blame Diana for her own tragic death. She is compared to a beautiful force of nature, requiring constant attention to be happy. These justifications do, however, conceal some unpleasant truths. Some sections of the press used free lance photographers, knowing full well that they were abusing the rights of Princess Diana. She was willing to be photographed when performing her public duties, but she asked the media to allow her some degree of privacy. Princess Diana understood the distinction between the public and the private. It is unfortunate that the distinction was ignored by the more intrusive press.

Privacy and the law

The extent of media intrusion into the private lives of individuals has led some people to argue in favour of a privacy law. This is regarded as a distinct threat by many in the media. It would curtail their activities and threaten their freedom. The threat of a privacy law is often used by governments in an attempt to curb irresponsible sections of the media. If the media could be relied upon to behave in a responsible manner, there would be less need for a privacy law. The media have thus had an active interest in reforming and policing themselves to avoid being constrained further by the law.

In 1949, the first Royal Commission on the press argued against a privacy law. As an alternative, it called for the formation of a General Council of the Press. The press were to provide its funds and 80% of its membership; the remaining 20% was to be drawn from outside the media. The General Council was to regulate the press, attempt to balance the freedom and responsibilities of the press, monitor the elite ownership and control of the press, and guard against increased secrecy in political life. The newspaper industry was, however, slow to implement these proposals. The Council did not meet for first time until July 1953[48].

---

[48] Snoddy, *The Good, the Bad and the Unacceptable*, pp83-84.

The General Council of the Press was regarded as ineffective in curbing poor behaviour, and this led to more discussions on a privacy law during the 1970s. The Younger Committee of 1970 concluded that it was impossible for the law to determine where the line should be drawn between the public and the private, and that the press should be left to decide for itself. In order to avoid abuse, an increasing percentage of the Press Council should be made up from people drawn from outside of the media. There was, however, minority support on the committee for a privacy law[49]. The McGregor Commission of 1974 attacked the press for publishing scurrilous material, and for invading the privacy of people. It argued that everybody should have a right to privacy, and that this should only be abridged if it could be shown to be in the public interest. The commission also showed how members of the press valued their own privacy. Its attempt to conduct a survey on the income and voting behaviour of members of the press was met with a barrage of criticism. It did not believe that the press should be subject to further legal regulation, but was willing to leave regulation to the Press Council[50].

This self regulatory approach was reinforced by the Calcutt Committee of 1990. It established the Press Complaints Commission to look into press intrusion (amongst other things) and emphasised the importance of journalists gaining the consent and permission of people they seeks to interview. The PCC Code of Conduct states that the press should respect the family, home, health and correspondence of the individual, unless the material can be shown to be in the 'public interest'[51]. This method of self regulation is preferred by many members of the press, who regard state intervention in general and a privacy law in particular as an unnecessary infringement upon the freedom of the press.

Journalists who favour a privacy law seem to be in a distinct minority. Alan Rusbridger, the editor of the *Guardian*, has argued that the government should take a stand on scandal mongering by the

---

[49] Snoddy, *The Good, the Bad and the Unacceptable*, p88.
[50] Snoddy, *The Good, the Bad and the Unacceptable*, p90.
[51] This is dealt with in more detail in chapter 1.

taboids. A privacy law could punish intrusive journalism, but still allow for serious investigative journalism. In this way, 'responsible journalism' could be encouraged[52]. Some academic commentators have argued that a legal right to privacy would not necessarily conflict with freedom of speech. The right to privacy refers to 'private facts in which there is no reasonable public interest', whilst freedom of speech refers to the discussion of public matters without being constrained by the state[53]. We are, of course, left with the problem of defining what is of public interest, but this must surely go beyond the 'interests of the public'.

There are numerous arguments against a legal right to privacy. Helen Searls, writing for the Marxist journal *LM*, has argued that Rusbridger over-emphasises the evils of the tabloids and the virtues of the quality press. She accuses Rusbridger and the *Guardian* of concentrating too much upon 'rather boring financial misdemeanours of yesterday's politicians' and claims that this '...hardly justifies Rusbridger's holier-than-thou demand for a privacy law'[54]. In her view, a legal right to privacy would hinder both freedom of speech and democratic debate. She claims that public figures invite the public into their lives and use their private lives to 'preach and moralise at us'. Given this, they can hardly complain when the public or the press scrutinise their lives. Searls believes that problems associated with intrusive tabloids are relatively small when compared with the dangers of a privacy law for '... the dangers of excluding a legitimate arena of discussion far outweigh the fact that individuals can suffer at the hands of a salacious press'[55].

Many members of the press (and other organisations) believe that they need to maintain the right to invade privacy in the public interest. This power is necessary in order to expose instances of political corruption. The *Independent on Sunday* has argued that the scandals

---

[52] Searls, 'The Rights and Wrongs of Privacy', p16.
[53] D. Richards, 'Free Speech as Toleration', p46 in W.J. Waluchow (ed), *Free Expression: Essays on Law and Philosophy*, Oxford University Press: Oxford, 1994, pp31-57.
[54] Searls, 'The Rights and Wrongs of Privacy', p17.
[55] Searls, 'The Rights and Wrongs of Privacy', p19.

involving the Thalidomide drug and the Soviet spy Kim Philby would not have been reported if a privacy law had been in place. Privacy legislation is also seen as a way for the establishment to cover its tracks. Relatively few 'ordinary people' are subject to such intense media scrutiny. The civil rights group Liberty go even further by arguing that privacy legislation would be most beneficial to the rich and the powerful, and warn that we need to know more (not less) about those who wield power. David Leigh, of the *Observer*, claims that it would be good if a privacy law could be drafted which would protect the ordinary citizen, but that a privacy law would almost certainly be used by 'crooked politicians' to prevent investigation into their activities[56]. Tom Bower points out that journalists cannot rely upon the legal system to regulate what is printed. His book on Robert Maxwell was suppressed in France under the privacy law because of its revelations about Maxwell's health. The same would have been the case in Britain if a privacy law was passed. Bower believes that a privacy law would inhibit serious investigative journalism, and that it is unrealistic to expect judges to protect free speech, freedom of the press and the activities of journalists against powerful interests[57].

For some commentators, a privacy law would undermine democracy. Andrew Belsey has argued that democracy needs freedom of expression and a free press, and that the press must be free to attack discrimination and bigotry, and uncover instances of corruption and fraud. The 'use and abuse of power' should not be concealed on the grounds of privacy. The British press is said to suffer from too many restrictions. A legal right to privacy would merely provide another weapon for those in positions of power to conceal their activities. He claims that privacy should be protected by ethics rather than by law. This could be enshrined within a new code

---

[56] M. Cloonan, 'The Press Part Three: Regulating the Press: The Calcutt Reports', *Case Studies for Politics 12*, University of York, pp4-5 and Welsh and Greenwood, *McNae's Essential Law for Journalists*, p267, and D. Leigh interviewed in *You Decide*, ITV, 5.08.1997.

[57] Tom Bower interviewed in *You Decide*, and Searls, 'The Rights and Wrongs of Privacy', p17.

of conduct which could emphasise the responsibilities of the press in a democratic society[58].

A privacy law would probably do something to curb irresponsible reporting, but quite possibly at a high price. It is argued that press intrusion into the lives of individuals is a reasonable price to pay for a free press. Those who argue against a privacy law do so by claiming that a free press is necessary to expose corruption, and to ensure that the powerful do not abuse our rights and threaten our liberties. It is thought that a privacy law would limit public discussion and threaten democracy. Although these are powerful arguments, they only work if the press is already behaving in a responsible manner. A responsible press would expose corruption and safeguard our interests. It is not enough to argue against a privacy law on the grounds that some sections of the media and some sections of the public want to invade the privacy of celebrities. Those members of the media who claim that a free press and broadcasting system is necessary for democracy should remind themselves of this before they consider invading the privacy of others.

Conclusion

The distinction between the public and the private is important in demarcating legitimate areas for the media to scrutinise. It is important that the media have free access to the public realm, to safeguard our interests and prevent abuses of power; but those in the public realm should also be entitled to privacy. In all self regarding matters, the individual should be free to determine what is private and what is of public concern. It has been recognised since the time of ancient Greece that people need to withdraw from their public duties, if only to re-charge and make themselves more effective in carrying out their social functions. Media intrusion into the private lives of public figures is rarely in the public interest. It might be in the 'interests of the public' to reveal intimate details about the lives of celebrities, but this does not make it in the 'public interest'. The

---

[58] Belsey, 'Privacy, Publicity and Politics', pp90-91.

`public interest' is concerned with the affairs of state. It is in the public interest to know those things which have direct bearing upon our rights and our lives. If the media pander to the interests of the public, it might do so at the expense of the public interest. It is, for example, more important to know about the policies of a government than about the sexual behaviour of a back-bencher. Whilst the `interests of the public' take precedence over the `public interest', it is possible for the government to exploit our apathy. A salacious media can harm democracy.

5. Racism

Racism involves holding negative views about people on the basis of the colour of their skin or their nationality. It is expressed in a variety of ways ranging from name calling, discrimination in economic and social life, excluding ethnic minorities from the corridors of power, through to violence motivated by hatred of other races. People are discriminated against when they are treated differently as a result of characteristics over which they have no control. Discriminating against somebody on the basis of their behaviour can be justified because there is an element of choice in the way we behave. Discrimination cannot be justified, however, on the basis of criteria beyond our control. This would include our racial background.

The origins of racism can be traced to a variety of sources. T.W. Adorno of the Frankfurt School, argued that those people holding racist views are more likely to be willing to subject themselves to authority, be aggressive towards those who refuse to subject themselves in this way, have a fear of outsiders, come from strict family backgrounds and hold strong religious views. Talcott Parsons attributes racism to cultural factors. He claims that a lot of racism is inherited through offensive assumptions, language and culture, which can be rectified by challenging such assumptions. It has also been argued that racism is systemic and is expressed in our institutions. It is often 'unconscious' and can only be rectified through a process of re-education (especially of public servants) and through positive discrimination[1].

The cultural and institutional explanations of racism do lend themselves to solutions. These solutions rely to a great extent upon the healing powers of education. If we accept that racism is unacceptable and intolerable, then we might consider challenging the uncharitable, politically incorrect or hostile assumptions we hold

---

[1] J. Rex, *Race and Ethnicity*, Open University Press: Milton Keynes, 1986, pp107-110.

about other races, and about their rights in the society within which we live. The cultural explanation shows that racism is built into our language. The terms white and black, for example, have often been used to denote good and bad respectively. Of course, we are not necessarily aware of our own racist attitudes. If we live in a culture which is in part defined by racist views, then racism can only be tackled through broad social, political (and possibly economic) change. Changing the language we use will have an effect, but not in isolation of more comprehensive reform.

If racism is the product of authoritarian personality traits, then the solution to the problem is far from straight forward. Those with authoritarian personalities are quite possibly rigid conformists who welcome discipline, seek power over others, and value such things as certainty, tradition and order. Short of subjecting these people to cultural shock therapy, there is little that can be done to shake their fear of outsiders and of lifestyles and/or experiences different from their own. It is unlikely, however, that racism can be attributed solely to certain personality traits. A person might be predisposed towards conformity, but that does not have to manifest itself in the holding of racist views. Dictatorships, which by definition encourage and rely upon high levels of conformity, have flourished throughout the world. Apart from in fascist systems (which tend to rest upon racist views), there is little reason to believe that incidences of racism are significantly greater in dictatorial states than in liberal democracies.

Racism in Britain stems primarily from the imperial traditions of the country. The legacy of empire perpetuated the assumption that white Britons were superior to black people from the former colonies, and this was reinforced by changes in the socio-economic system where upwardly mobile whites left relatively low paid work and were replaced by black workers. The British education system promoted stereotyped views of colonial life which did little to alleviate prejudice. Overt racism, however, was seen as incompatible with traditional British values concerning human rights and equality of treatment. This contradiction, it has been argued, caused `... the great majority of people to feel uneasy about the direct expression of racialist ideas'[2]. It is clear, however, that forms of racism are enshrined within the British social and political system. This chapter is concerned with the role of the media in perpetuating racist views. It looks at the ways in which the media express racist views and the access of racist groups to the media.

Racism and the media

According to Stuart Hall, racism is a distinct and wide-ranging ideology which rests upon the belief that black people are a `problem' which white people have to solve. Although there is overt and easily identifiable racism in some of the partisan press, there is also a widespread and concealed racism which permeates broadcasting in Britain. This was described as `inferential racism' and can be found where racist arguments are presented as `common sense' or `unquestioned assumptions'; this, in turn, serves as a platform for overt racism. Inferential racism, according to Hall, is quite common and he believes that it is `... more insidious, because it is largely invisible to those who formulate the world in its terms'[3]. This racism is perpetuated in the media through the use of stereotypes and in selective news coverage of ethnic minorities. What follows will concentrate in particular upon media representations of black people.

Racist messages are presented through the use of distinct language and images. This involves concealing the historical roots of the structures of power which pervade relations between races. The racist ideology suggests that relations of subordination and domination are fixed, and that they are expressions of natural superiority and inferiority. The use of stereotypes allows for ethnic minorities to be presented as both a source of fun and of danger. In the so-called `old'

---

[2] M. and A. Dummett, `The Role of Government in Britain's Racial Crisis', p113 in C. Husband (ed), *Race in Britain: Continuity and Change*, Hutchinson Education: London, 1987, pp111-141. See also: Rex, *Race and Ethnicity*, p105.

[3] S. Hall, `Racist Ideologies and the Media', p162 in P. Marris and S. Thornham (eds), *Media Studies: A Reader*, Edinburgh University Press: Edinburgh, 1996, pp160-168.

images of race, there were three main stereotypes: the *slave figure*, the *native* and the *entertainer*. The *slave figure* was portrayed as having child-like devotion and love, whilst being unreliable, unpredictable and liable to `turn nasty'. The *native* could be dignified and noble, but also cunning and liable to cheat. The *entertainer* was less malevolent. This stereotype had `innate humour' and physical grace . Such images continue in contemporary culture. Black people are still portrayed as `restless natives', crooks and threats to civilisation[4].

Sexual stereotypes have been particularly prevalent in media portrayals of black people. In 1992, for example, the *Sun* published a feature on the runner Linford Christie which asked readers to guess what was in his `lunch box'. It said that Christie's `... skin tight lycra shorts hide little as he pounds down the track and his Olympic-sized talents are a source of delight for women around the world. But the mystery remains - just what does Linford, 32, pack in that famous lunchbox'[5]. It has been argued that the feature, which Christie dismissed as harmless, was aimed at a predominantly white male audience and invoked the image of black men as hyper-sexual threats to white women[6].

What is seen as racism changes over time and depends a great deal on context. Quintin Tarantino has recently been criticised by Spike Lee for his apparent obsession with using the term `nigger' in his films. He used the term 28 times in *Pulp Fiction* and 38 times in *Jackie Brown*. Spike Lee also uses the word nigger but, given that he is a black director, its political force is rather different. When a white person like Tarantino directs black people to use the term, it can be tinged with racism. Tarantino remains adamant, however, that he is not afraid to use the word and that he does want to be limited by `white guilt' or feel like `pussyfooting around racial issues'[7]. If racism could be traced simply to the language that is used, it would be

---

[4]   Hall, `Racist Ideologies and the Media', pp164-165.

[5]   The *Sun*, 6.8.1992 cited in J. Solomos and L. Back, *Racism and Society*, Macmillan: London, 1996, p193.

[6]   Solomos and Back, *Racism and Society*, p193.

[7]   Quintin Tarantino cited in P. Sawyers, `Screen: Don't mention the N word', *Guardian*, 20.03.1998.

relatively easy to monitor racist messages in the media and rectify blatant discrimination and racial abuse. Racism can be detected, however, in the selective representation of ethnic minorities in the press and broadcasting.

It has been argued that the press tend to define ethnic minorities as a problem rather than deal with the problems facing minority communities. Ethnic minorities often feature in the news when they are thought to pose a problem to the white population[8]. During the 1960s, for example, the British media presented an image of the black population as a social problem. It was assumed that racial problems were *caused* by immigration. Black people were regarded as 'interlopers', who would not be here for long and who were living in small enclaves. No attempt was made to understand black life. Instead, the media concentrated upon any incidents of crime. Current affairs programmes tied ethnic minorities to public health scares, to racial tension and to the fear of more immigration. This fear of the black community in particular has continued to feature in media coverage of ethnic minorities[9].

During the 1970s, the black population was portrayed as different and problematic. Very few black people got to express their own views in the media, and those that did tended to be those who were 'successful' and had embraced the values of the white middle class[10]. In May 1976, a story broke in the tabloids which depicted refugees from Malawi in a bad light. The headlines suggested that they were 'scroungers'. The *Sun* ran a story entitled 'Scandal of £600 a week immigrants'. The story referred to a group of Asian refugees who had been placed, temporarily, in a hotel with a rent of £600 a week. Within a week, the *Daily Mail* published a story called 'We want

[8] Van Dijk cited in J. Watson, *Media Communication*, Macmillan: Houndmills, 1998, p172.
[9] Stuart Hall interview shown in *Race Portrayal*, BBC2, 6.10.1996, and S. Cottle, 'Ethnic Minorities in the British News Media', p193 in J. Stokes and A. Reading (eds), *The Media in Britain*, Macmillan: Houndmills, 1999, pp191-199.
[10] J. Thackara, 'The Mass Media and Racism' p109 in C. Gardner (ed), *Media, Politics and* Culture, Macmillan: London, 1979, pp108-118.

more money, say the £600 a week Asians'. Peter Evans, of the *Times*, argued that this story worked because it drew upon four popularly help notions. It suggested that immigrants live off the state, that welfare services are inept, that such 'sponging' harms Britain's economic prospects and that state aid in general bleeds the nation of resources. According to Evans, the media frenzy did not stem from a deliberate racist campaign but from the tendency of news stories to gain momentum of their own and from '... a mounting clamour that excites the senses and can sometimes drown the still small voice of reason'[11]. John Thackara disagrees with this appraisal. He argues that this in no way justifies the behaviour of the media, and that the media behaved in an appalling way by creating a climate of opinion for racists to exploit[12].

Racist messages can also be seen in media coverage of so-called 'race riots'. It is often assumed that the police interpretation of a demonstration is correct. Coverage of the causes of the 'riot' are '... either missing, or introduced so late in the process of signification, that they fail to dislodge the dominant definition of these events'[13]. Such was the case in the media coverage of demonstrations in Southall during the early 1980s. The media turned the conflict between racism and anti-racism into one between the Asian population and the police, and between the extreme right and the extreme left. This ignored the problem of the rise of the right, the growth of racism, and of racism in the police force. By concentrating upon the conflict between extremes (the National Front and the Anti-Nazi League), the media cast itself as moderate and presented both the left and right as equally to blame[14].

It is argued that the press during the 1980s was highly selective in its presentation of the life of ethnic minorities. The press continued to concentrate on questions of immigration, discrimination and race riots, but virtually ignored the contributions made by minority groups

---

[11] Peter Evans cited in Thackara, 'The Mass Media and Racism', p110.
[12] Thackara, 'The Mass Media and Racism', pp110-111.
[13] Hall, 'Racist Ideologies and the Media', p166.
[14] Hall, 'Racist Ideologies and the Media', pp166-167.

to politics, social affairs and culture. The press have been accused of treating ethnic minorities as 'invisible' until they do something to shake the system and allow the press to define ethnic minorities as a problem. Sections of the press reflect white society, perpetuate a white consensus, and do little to spread good news about ethnic minorities[15]. Some sections of the press are known to take into account the racism of their audience when making editorial decisions. Even if individual reporters do not harbour such views, many news organisations will consider the 'market orientation' and supposed views of their audience. It is said, for example, that the *Sun* is loathe to print good news about ethnic minorities and that it is '... the last thing our readers want, pictures of blacks raking it in'[16].

The media often seem to concentrate too much upon the problems *caused by* rather than the problems *faced by* ethnic minorities. In extreme cases, this sometimes involves 'demonising' minorities. The *Bristol Evening Post*, for example, ran a front page story in April 1996 under the title of 'Faces of Evil'. This was accompanied by 16 police photographs of convicted drug dealers, all of whom were black. It has been argued that this was a deliberately sensationalist story which neglected to deal with real problems associated with the rise of drug dealing, and with any other information about the black population. The crime of drug dealing was said to be 'racialised' by an editorial staff which might not have considered sixteen white faces to be of front page significance[17]. Racist messages can also be found in media coverage of foreign affairs. Zeinab Badawi claims that the way black people are portrayed in foreign news has an impact upon the way that black people are viewed in Britain. She believes that broadcasters must be aware of the effects of their commentary, and whether they are likely to reinforce racist attitudes. Negative images are reinforced by the selection of stories. Badawi complains about the

---

[15] Watson, *Media Communication*, p174.

[16] This comment was attributed to a member of the *Sun*'s editorial team. Cited in Cottle, 'Ethnic Minorities and the British News Media', p194. See also p 195.

[17] Cottle, 'Ethnic Minorities and the British News Media', pp192-193.

'coup, war, famine syndrome' in which stories about Africa will only appear in the news if one of these events occur. Such things are certainly worthy of coverage, but these images must be shown in a broader context[18].

Violence against minority races is often under-reported. In 1991, for example, social unrest on housing estates in Oxford, Tyneside and Cardiff was presented in the media as a battle between police and youths. It focused upon the spectacular; joy riding and cars on fire. What the media failed to cover was that Asian shopkeepers were subject to violence on the estates, and that some had been bombed out of their homes[19]. Giving the impression that ethnic minorities are a 'problem for white society' not only reinforces racist views, but can also have a devastating effect upon the civil rights of significant sections of the British population. The Stephen Lawrence case illustrates that negative images of black people can contribute towards negligent and prejudicial policing, and distort the judicial system. When the Crown Prosecution Service was unable to make a case against a group of youths accused of killing Lawrence, it was left to his parents to fight for justice. This was seen as indicative of the authority's failure to protect the black community[20]. Minority races are subject to increasing physical violence. In 1991, for example, there were somewhere in the region of 53,000 racial threats, 26,000 incidents of racially motivated vandalism and 32,000 incidents of racial assaults. It is estimated that there is an average of 100 racial assaults per day and that there are approximately 100,000 people in Britain committing racist acts. This activity is, however, 'consistently under-reported'[21].

---

[18] Zeinab Badawi interview shown in *Race Portrayal*.

[19] Rosalind Brunt interviewed in *Open Saturday: Hype, hysteria and fluffy business'*, BBC 1, 29.8.1998.

[20] For further details see J. Owen, 'Documentary and Citizenship: The Case of Stephen Lawrence', p201 in J. Stokes and A. Reading (eds), *The Media in Britain*, Macmillan: Houndmills, 1999, pp201-207.

[21] B. Cathcart, 'Real Britannia: It starts with name calling. Where does it end?', *Independent*, 23.7.1998.

Part of the problem lies in the lack of black journalists. During the 1970s, only 0.1% of the National Union of Journalists were black. White reporters were often not able to deal with issues relating to the immigrant community because of language barriers, and there were cases of papers confusing nationalities and religions to such a degree that the stories made little sense to the immigrant community[22]. Journalism remains a predominantly white occupation. In 1994, it was estimated that there were only 20 black or Asian journalists (out of a total of 4000 journalists) working for national newspapers. In the provincial press, there were only 15 out of 8000. Broadcasting fared considerably better. Equal opportunities policies, especially those run by the BBC, have increased the number of black and Asian people involved in broadcasting; but over half of the black staff work on programmes designed for a black target group[23].

Workers in the media have been active in combating racist views. The Campaign Against Racism in the Media (CARM) was established in the 1970s to push for black representation in the media and for a more rounded image of black life. It was formed in reaction to tabloid headlines that were thought to be inciting racial hatred. CARM set out to exert pressure on those responsible for producing racist messages. It took an active stand against fascism, rather than attempting to remain 'neutral' on race issues, and took part in anti-racist pickets[24]. CARM used community pressure against newspapers thought to be reporting race issues in an irresponsible way. It's campaign was fought on a national and local level. The *Tottenham Herald*, for example, had printed such headlines as 'Black Girl's Brutal Attack on Home Help' and 'What About Us Whites Asks Angry Councillor'. CARM responded by arranging a meeting between itself, journalists from the paper and black groups in the community. Although the *Herald* journalists argued that a paper in a

---

[22] Thackara, 'The Mass Media and Racism', p113.

[23] Cottle, 'Ethnic Minorities and the British News Media', p195.

[24] *Race Portrayal* and G. Sheridan, 'CARM, race and the media: The story so far', in P. Cohen and C. Gardner (eds), *It aint half racist mum*, Comedia: London, 1982, pp1-4.

racist community cannot avoid reporting racist news, the journalists backed down when they were told of the extent of racial discrimination and abuse in the community[25].

Racist messages still appear in the media with relatively little resistance. Simon Cottle has identified a number of key factors which go towards explaining the perpetuation of racism in the media. He claims that the notion of objectivity has tended to dissuade journalists from championing the cause of ethnic minorities and thus it has helped to reinforce the white consensus. Market pressures have marginalised features on the lives and achievements of ethnic minorities, whilst sensationalising problems in race relations. The media have been slow to ask ethnic minority groups for their opinions, and have relied upon more traditional centres of power when researching stories. There also remains a deep seated view that stories about ethnic minorities should be about racial conflict, crime and violence. These news values help to perpetuate imbalance in the way that ethnic minorities are portrayed in the media[26].

Racist messages are codified in the media and often passed off as common sense. Racism portrays the black population as a problem for the white population to solve. The media often concentrate upon black crime, benefit fraud and 'race riots' and neglect to mention anything positive about ethnic minorities. It is argued that black people are virtually excluded from media coverage until they are thought to pose a threat to white society. This does not mean that negative news should be excluded. Jim Rose, the chair of Penguin Books, argues that although racism harms the prospects for peace between the different races of Britain, this should not be used as an excuse by journalists to suppress or censor news which portray the immigrant community in a bad light. This form of 'censorship' is considered 'inconsistent with the freedom of the press'[27]. Thackara believes that journalists should attempt neither to be neutral nor

---

[25] Thackara, 'The Mass Media and Racism', p115.
[26] Cottle, 'Ethnic Minorities in the British News Media', pp196-197.
[27] See Rose comments and Thackara's reply in Thackara, 'The Mass Media and Racism', p116.

impartial about racism, as the publication of racist views merely reinforces racism in society. Racism deserves critical coverage. According to Thackara, journalists should be `... both objective *and* biased, reporting the true facts about the situation of blacks in Britain today, some of which will come as an unpleasant surprise to many people, but also explaining the roots of racism and how the racist parties are exploiting it for their own anti-freedom ends'[28]. It is important to undermine the view that black people per se are a problem. To assume that ethnic minorities are a problem and that the correct interpretation of events is always presented by the predominantly white establishment is, by its very nature, a racist assumption. Individuals are not necessarily to blame for these images. It is not because those in the media intend to be racist, but that the media function in an environment defined in part (and constrained by) a complex and deep-seated racist ideology[29]. It would seem important, therefore, to challenge this ideology.

The media and racist groups

The British political system has adapted to racism in a piecemeal way. For many years, racism was not regarded widely as a problem. It was, if anything, part of the imperial mentality; and was thus acceptable in terms of the dominant values of the age. The decline of empire and increases in immigration, however, transformed the way that many British people regarded non-white races. During the 1960s and 1970s, Labour governments attempted to legislate against racial discrimination. This (though not in isolation of other economic and social factors) contributed towards divisions in the Conservative Party. Enoch Powell offered a doomsday scenario to the British people in which white Britons were intimidated, sent to prison or run out of their homes by an ever increasing immigrant community. This vision proved to be a source of embarrassment to the Conservative left who tended to regard racism as incompatible with the British tradition

---

[28] Thackara, `The Mass Media and Racism', p117.
[29] Hall, `Racist Ideologies and the Media', p168.

and thus unacceptable. The extreme right exploited this division until the late 1970s when Mrs. Thatcher closed the gap by adopting mild racist views[30].

Racist politics were intensified in 1967 with the formation of the National Front. The National Front existed on the fringes of the Conservative Party for many years. It recruited those sympathetic to Enoch Powell's conservatism, and managed to infiltrate the Conservative Monday Club during the early 1970s. The National Front attacked both the Jewish and Black communities of Britain. Like the Nazis, the Front believed that there was an international Jewish conspiracy. It claimed that the Jews were attempting to dominate the world by encouraging inter-racial breeding whilst forbidding Jews to marry outside their own ethnic group. The Jews were thought to control the media and this explained the portrayal of anti-nationalist, anti-racist and anti-fascist images. The black community was attacked and labelled as intellectually and culturally inferior. It was argued that white Britons were superior to all other groups of people. This superiority was threatened by breeding with other races, which diluted the racial stock. The National Front believed that immigration was the source of Britain's socio-economic problems during the 1970s[31].

Between 1973 and 1976, the National Front prospered in elections. In the West Bromwich by-election of 1973, the Front gained 16% of the vote. In the General Election of October 1974, it received a total of 113,579 votes divided between 90 candidates. This made it England's fourth largest party. This was followed by some notable successes in Blackburn and Leicester in the local elections of 1976[32]. In addition to its participation in elections, the Front attempted to recruit support by the use of provocative marches into predominantly

---

[30] For a series of accounts on race in British politics see Husband (ed), *Race in Britain: Continuity and Change.*

[31] B. Troyna, 'Reporting Racism: The British Way of Life Observed', p282 in Husband (ed), *Race in Britain: Continuity and Change*, pp275-291, M. Barker, *The New Racism*, Junction Books: London, 1981, pp25-26, and P. Dorey, *British Politics Since 1945*, Blackwell: Oxford, 1995, p142.

[32] Dorey, *British Politics Since 1945*, p143.

black or Jewish areas . This tactic gave rise to counter demonstrations led, at first, by the International Marxist Group. In 1974, violence resulted, one of the counter-demonstrators was killed and the police intervened to protect the National Front. The Front began to emphasise its right to march regardless of opposition and claimed that it was the true upholder of the right of assembly[33].

The National Front claimed to be the champion of free speech, and demanded that it have access to the media to spread its views in party political broadcasts. This was opposed by various anti-racist groups. In August 1976, some people from the Socialist Workers' Party set up Rock Against Racism. This organisation invited those involved in music to unite against and declare their opposition to racism. This was a response to the overtly racist and/or fascist declarations by some of the most respected names in rock music; including Eric Clapton's support for Enoch Powell, and David Bowie's claim that Hitler was the `first superstar' and that Britain needed a right wing dictatorship. The Rock Against Racism movement attracted support from the new wave of punk bands; many of whom wedded anti-racist and anti-establishment politics. There were, however, some sections of the punk movement which (intentionally or not) gained support from the fascist movement. The National Front had its own counter movement (Rock Against Communism) which applauded the Stranglers' `I Feel Like a Wog' and Clash's `White Man in Hammersmith Palais'[34]. Rock Against Racism was a grass roots movement. It attracted young bands determined to topple some of the icons of rock with their own blend of aggressive street music. It did, however, lack a co-ordinated and coherent campaign. The strength of Rock Against Racism lay in its simple anti-racist message.

In November 1977, anti-racist politics changed direction with the launch of the Anti Nazi League (ANL). This was a broad based movement (rather like CND) which sought to unite anti-fascist

---

[33]   Troyna, `Reporting Racism: The British Way of Life Observed', pp284-285 and Whitehead, *The Writing on the Wall*, p231.
[34]   P. Gilroy, *There Aint No Black in the Union Jack*, Hutchinson: London, 1987, pp120-124.

opinion regardless of other political differences. The ANL argued that the National Front were proponents of sham patriotism and that Britain's true national greatness could be seen in the 1939-45 war against fascism. Rather than directing their fervour towards undermining racism, the ANL wanted to limit political support for the National Front. Racism was viewed as a by-product of fascism rather than in its own right. The ANL sought to attract older members (perhaps with memories of the war) and women (by emphasising fascist subordination of women) rather than concentrate solely upon young rock fans. Its activities, however, did much to undermine the appeal of the original Rock Against Racism movement[35].

The ANL wanted, amongst other things, to limit the National Front's access to the media. By putting up over fifty candidates at the General Election, the National Front was entitled to a five minute political broadcast. Peter Hain, on behalf of the ANL, wrote to the BBC in September 1978 calling for a ban on the proposed election broadcast and for silent treatment of their electioneering. Hain argued that the National Front should be deprived of publicity because they stand for `... a form of racial ideology that threatens the freedom of biologically defined groups not only to speak, but also to be'[36]. This was supported by Sheridan and Gardner, of the Campaign Against Racism in the Media (CARM), who argued that the National Front should not be given access to the media because its speeches incited violence against black people. They compared it to allowing media time to somebody who advocated dangerous driving, and claimed that journalists must be made subject to the National Union of Journalists code of conduct which forbade encouraging discrimination `on grounds of race, colour, creed, gender or sexual orientation'[37].

Ian Threthowan, speaking on behalf of the BBC, refused Hain's request stating that all legally constituted parties must be treated

---

[35] Gilroy, *There aint no black in the Union Jack* , pp131-133.
[36] Peter Hain cited in Troyna, `Reporting Racism: The British Way of Life Observed', p283.
[37] G. Sheridan and C. Gardner, `Press Freedom: A Socialist Strategy', p131 in C. Gardner (ed), *Media, Politics and Culture*, Macmillan: London, 1979. See also pp130-131.

equally. Michael Swann, chair of the BBC, said that the BBC could not suppress the broadcast for it would `... be a negation of those principles of freedom of speech that we have fought for so long ... freedom of speech must be indivisible'[38]. For the ANL, freedom of speech was not an absolute value. It made little sense to support the rights of the fascists when their activities threaten the freedom of considerable numbers in society. The response of the BBC shows that if we are truly supporters of freedom of speech, it is important to extend that right to the entire spectrum of political opinion regardless of whether a group embraces or rejects tolerance of other views.

Anti-racist groups have been accused of being aggressive and intolerant. Lord Hailsham, for example, felt that the National Front was a `thoroughly detestable organisation' but that the `still nastier Socialist Workers' Party' were motivated not simply by a hatred of fascism but by the desire `... to dictate by means of their strong arm tactics who should and who should not be allowed to organise and demonstrate in this supposedly free country'[39]. Many of the newspapers on the right and centre of the political spectrum had similar things to say. The *Daily Express* warned of the `fascist left' and felt that right wing groups were more passionate about liberty and the rule of law. The *Daily Telegraph* supported the rights of the National Front to march in `their capital' regardless of whether `it is settled by immigrants'. Even the *Observer* felt that right wing groups, however detestable, had the right to the same level of freedom as other organisations[40]. Such criticisms point out that some anti-racist groups adopt tactics more suited to the right. Racism should not be (and ultimately cannot be) dealt with adequately by intolerance, aggression and censorship.

The debate over the freedom of racist organisations continues in the 1990s. In April 1994, Paul Foot criticised the *Independent* for

---

[38] Michael Swann cited in Troyna, `Reporting Racism: The British way of life observed', p284.

[39] Hailsham cited in Troyna, `Reporting Racism: The British Way of Life Observed', p286.

[40] Troyna, `Reporting Racism: The British Way of Life Observed', p286.

printing a letter from the British National Party. He claimed that the '... normal rules of free speech and expression cannot possibly apply to those who aim to deny the most basic rights and freedoms to entire sections of the population'[41]. *The Independent* argued that it would be politically dangerous to ignore the views of the BNP, given that it was gaining support in Tower Hamlets and because of the resurgence of right wing parties. It is important to recognise that the BNP was gaining support not by virtue of its ideology, but because it was a symptom of serious problems which the main political parties were failing to deal with. The *Independent* argued that it is far more important to reveal the causes of the problems, rather than attempt to suppress its symptoms[42]. Andrew Marr of the *Independent* claims that we have a duty to listen to what he calls 'muttonheads' because freedom of speech is '... precious because it allows society to self-correct by applying human reason to any problem'[43].

It is still a matter for debate whether racist groups should have access to the media. Writing in the *Guardian* on the eve of the 1997 General Election, Michael Mansfield argued that the BNP should not be allowed to have its broadcast because the party is hostile towards democracy, it incites hatred towards ethnic minorities which encourages racial attacks, and because there is a very thin line between saying and doing[44]. Donu Kogbara argued against banning the broadcast for fear that such a precedent could be used to ban 'views that we do like'. She claimed that she was saddened by the existence of racist views but that '... as long as they don't actually tell their audiences to harm black people or property, BNP morons who loathe me should be entitled to chant their vile slogans on any public platform'[45]. She claimed that racism cannot be eradicated through censorship. The law should punish illegal acts carried out by the

---

[41] Paul Foot cited in 'Liberalism can cope with the skinheads', *Independent*, 16.4.1994.

[42] 'Liberalism can cope with the skinheads'.

[43] Andrew Marr, 'A duty to hear muttonheads', *Independent*, 14.4.1994.

[44] Mansfield in M. Mansfield and D. Kogbara, 'Speech of Freedom', *Guardian*, 19.4.1997.

[45] Kogbara in Mansfield and Kogbara, 'Speech of Freedom'.

group and monitor their activities carefully. It was therefore better that they express their views in the open. We can't watch what we can't see. She believed, moreover, that if the BNP was censored `... you give them a fascinating mystique and turn them into a slightly glamorous `persecuted' minority'[46]. The liberal mind is apt to create victims out of those deprived of freedom of speech .

It has long been the case that the expression of racist views has been justified on the grounds of freedom of speech. The British political culture sometimes seems more tolerant of the extreme right than it is of the extreme left. British law forbids the use of words designed to stir up racial hatred, but does not forbid the expression of racist views. Some anti-racist groups have argued that racists should be denied access to the media, and that the principles of freedom of speech should not apply to those who would deprive significant sections of the population of their basic civil rights. Censoring such views from the mainstream media would, however, be self-defeating. It would create martyrs out of racist groups, and could undermine attempts by anti-racist factions to promote a more balanced appreciation of the lives of ethnic minorities. Many members of ethnic minorities will have experience of dealing with discrimination and racial abuse. This is often orchestrated by racist groups. The more we understand racists, the more insight we can have into some of the problems *faced by* ethnic minorities. Censorship will do nothing in itself to overturn the ideological system which scapegoats members of different races.

Conclusion

The extreme right must be granted the same democratic rights as other political groups. Depriving the BNP of access to the media would do little to remove the causes of racism and make such groups even more secretive and dangerous. The media can serve the public interest more fully by monitoring these groups and reminding us of the threat they pose to ethnic minorities, women and democracy. The

---

[46]   Kogbara, `Speech of Freedom'.

selective media portrayal of black people does more harm to race relations than the occasional utterances of extreme right parties. The media perpetuate racism by presenting the black population as a problem, by using offensive stereotypes, and by focusing on the problems caused by ethnic minorities rather than the problems they face. Prejudicial coverage of ethnic minorities not only harms race relations, but also provides a misleading diagnosis of social and economic ills. News organisations can and do reform themselves by showing due respect for balanced reporting. News of ethnic minorities should be placed in proper context. Groups representing ethnic minorities should be consulted when researching stories, rather than relying upon the views of the predominantly white establishment. Racism should not be ignored, but subjected to critical coverage.

6. Sexism

Sexism involves the prejudicial treatment of one gender by another, or action by one gender designed to demean another. The term is often used in western societies to refer to the power held by men over women. Sexist acts include such things as discriminating against women in economic, social and political life, and the holding and promotion of views that negate the contribution made by women to society and present women as naturally subordinate domestic or sexual `commodities' for the pleasure of men[1]. The term sexism was introduced to modern language by feminist writers and activists. Feminists make their principal appeal to gender, they concentrate upon tracing the roots of the subordination of women, and suggest ways for women to liberate themselves from the constraints of patriarchal society. For some, this involves a policy of equal opportunities, others look to undo the bonds between men and women, whilst for others the liberation of women cannot take place in isolation from a fundamental social and economic transformation of society. They argue that gender roles and identities are not pre-ordained but are socially determined[2]. Given this, the relative subordination of women can be overcome.

A key feature of the feminist argument is to be found in its rejection of the traditional liberal distinction between the public and private spheres. Susan Okin has pointed out that liberals want to protect the private sphere from social and governmental intervention. This `private sphere' is often equated with `domestic' life. Women are thought to inhabit this private sphere, whilst men assume control of the public realms of economic and political life. With this control, men grant themselves political rights and the right to control their own household. The feminist response is to declare that the `personal is political'. This means that personal relationships are political

[1] See D. Robertson, *Dictionary of Politics*, Penguin: Harmondsworth, 1993, pp434-435.
[2] S. Rowbotham, *The Past is Before Us*, Pandora: London, 1989, p113.

because they involve an element of power. Feminists have thus sought to challenge power relations within the family so as to transform gender roles. This refusal to accept the liberal distinction between the public and the private has also led some feminists to argue that the domestic sphere should be open to state intervention[3].

In addition to transforming family relations, it is clear that many feminists want greater access to the 'public' sphere. Under a system of liberal democracy, there is the assumption that we all have equal access to power. This ignores inequalities in the relative power of men and women. This inequality exists at both an elite level (noted by the absence of women in key positions, relative to men) and at the mass level were women have endured exclusion from the public realm and have tended to be passive as citizens. Liberal democracy thus promises autonomy and self-determination, but fails to deliver because women are often excluded from the exercise of power. It has been argued that women are less likely to participate in politics for they are often constrained by the demands of the private sphere. Inequalities in the sexual division of labour (especially in child rearing) militate against women entering the public sphere. The private sphere thus has a direct effect upon levels of participation in the public sphere. The political and intellectual system are controlled by men and dominated by a male agenda. Women are, therefore, encouraged by many feminists to form their own groups to deal with their own issues rather than to compete with men for power within patriarchal institutions[4].

Media portrayal of women

The media have had a particularly important role in maintaining the relative subordination of women. Writing in the 1930s, Virginia Woolf claimed that the way the press presented the news showed that

---

[3] S.M. Okin, 'Gender, the Public and the Private', pp68-77 in D. Held (ed), *Political Theory Today*, Polity: Cambridge, 1991, pp67-90.
[4] See J. Schwarzmantel, *The State in Contemporary Society*, Harvester: Hemel Hempstead, 1994, pp114-116, and 123-126.

Britain was a patriarchal society. Public affairs were considered to be masculine and of more importance than feminine issues of sexuality and recreation[5]. A similar impression of the patriarchal character of the media endured into the 1970s, when it was argued that male domination of the media reinforced the view that men are active and creative, whereas women are effectively the audience for male activity[6].

Men continue to dominate the news. Research conducted in the United States showed that in 1993 men were the central figures in 85% of American news stories, and provided 75% of sources for network news. Men accounted for 86% of correspondents, and were assigned *hard* news stories (those dealing with the public sector), whereas women were given *soft* stories (dealing with social services and family issues)[7]. Sue Jansen claims that the gender split in the coverage of news occurs because there exists a widely held assumption that it is more `manly' to deal with issues of war and violence than with social problems[8].

The same trends are found in Britain. According to Patricia Holland, women appear and speak in news bulletins less than men. Women tend neither to be the central character in a news item, nor do they get selected to provide expert opinion on news items. Instead, women appear as examples of un-informed public opinion, or as victims of a particular crime or government policy. They tend to `... speak as passive reactors and witnesses to public events rather than as participants in those events'[9]. The news agenda is distinctly patriarchal. According to Holland, the news is presented in a non-emotional way, and subordinates the `private sphere' to the public sphere. As men tend to occupy more senior posts in the social,

[5]   Virginia Woolf cited in M. Merck, `Sexism in the Media ?', p107 in C. Gardner (ed), *Media, Politics and Culture*, Macmillan: London, 1979, pp95-107.
[6]   Merck, `Sexism in the Media ?', p103.
[7]   Watson, *Media Communication*, p171.
[8]   Sue Jansen cited in Watson, *Media Communication*, p171.
[9]   P. Holland, `When a woman reads the news', p197 in H. Baehr and A. Gray (eds), *Turning it on*, Arnold: London, 1996, pp195-199.

economic and political systems, the news deals with their stories and thereby excludes many women. Women are thus `... expelled from the imagery of the news just as they are expelled from those areas of public life from which the news is derived'[10].

The tabloids, in particular, are prone to caricature the lives of women and exclude women from the news unless they are performing `motherly' or protective roles or in sex scandals. Teresa Stratford has argued that `... tabloid editors and owners are distinctly uncomfortable with issues of sex and sexuality; only by sensationalising and caricaturing such issues can they deal with them'[11]. This highly selective portrayal of women, which focuses upon women's sexuality rather than their intellectual abilities, can be seen in the overt sexual imagery contained in some newspapers, the way that lesbians are treated by the press, the tabloid preoccupation with rape, and in the slanted portrayal of feminism and the women's movement.

In 1986, The Labour MP Clare Short introduced her Indecent Displays Act which sought to make it illegal for newspapers to include pictures of naked people in sexually provocative poses. This became known as the `Page 3 Bill', after the infamous page 3 of The Sun newspaper. It sought, not to censor, but to re-define the nature of newspapers. The tabloids, especially The Sun, turned on Clare Short and launched the `Crazy Clare' campaign to imply that she was not quite sane, and the Tory government made sure that her proposals were never passed into law[12]. The quest, however, continued with the launching in the House of Commons of the Campaign Against Pornography in January 1988. This group was responsible for, amongst other things, the `Off the Shelf' campaign which exerted pressure upon W.H. Smith to stop distributing pornographic magazines[13].

---

[10] Holland, `When a woman reads the news', p198. See also p197.
[11] T. Stratford, `Women and the press', p131 in A. Belsey and R. Chadwick (eds), *Ethical Issues in Journalism and the Media*, Routledge: London, 1992, pp130-136.
[12] T. Stratford, `Women and the Press' p132.
[13] `Chronology of Anti-Pornography Initiatives in the UK', p592 and p595 in C. Itzin (ed), *Pornography*, OUP: Oxford, 1992, pp589-597.

It has been argued that `page 3' has become a kind of institution which confirms a subordinate place for women in society. The editors of tabloids point out that there are more applicants for this form of modelling than they can possibly use. This work serves, moreover, as an escape route for some working class women. Stratford points out, however, that the packaging of `page 3' is or can be demeaning. She illustrates that the models are used as symbols of female sexuality and are seen as `sexually available'. They are presented as open and friendly, though with `a mother's large, nurturing breasts', and often alongside a caption suggesting that they are `tasty', `luscious' or in some other way good to eat. According to Statford, it is `... this aspect of the Page 3 phenomenon which women find most demeaning, and it is so far from the realities of most women's lives to be anachronistic, a comforting habit retained by the men who run the newspapers to remind themselves daily that the power balance still lies in their favour'[14].

The Sun is in the process of changing its policy towards page 3. In recent times, the editorial team of the paper has turned its attention to attracting more women readers. Rebekah Wade, the deputy editor, has argued that it is important for the paper to maintain its `sexy image', but this can be done with pictures of women with at least some clothes on. The declining circulation of the paper has forced it to reassess its policies. Between January 1997 and January 1998, *The Sun* lost approximately 5% of its readership. The National Readership Survey has found that a significant percentage of women moved from reading the *Sun* to reading the *Mail*[15]. Similar papers have also been forced to reform their content and tone. The *Daily Star* lost a lot of advertising revenue because of its increased coverage of sexual issues[16].

It would appear that feminist ideas in particular have had an effect upon social attitudes towards page 3. Clare Short's campaign did not

---

[14]   Stratford, `Women and the Press', p133.

[15]   K. Ahmed, `Sun to spend £ 2.5 m to woo back readers', *Guardian*, 28.2.1998. p10.

[16]   Snoddy, *The Good, the Bad and the Unacceptable*, p99.

succeed in changing the law or forcing editors to reconsider the manner in which they portrayed women. It is quite possible, however, that it raised awareness amongst women readers about the outdated images contained on page 3. Market pressure has forced British newspapers (and magazines) to review their policies. Short argued that pornographic images were inappropriate in newspapers. She did not advocate the wholesale censoring of all pornographic images and of sexually explicit speech. Her intention was to shift this into a specialised market and thereby effect a transformation in mainstream values.

The press play an active part in promoting sexual images of women, and in marginalising those who refuse to conform to these images. Ten percent of the population in Britain is homosexual yet heterosexuality is still treated as the norm and when gays are mentioned it is usually a term confined to describe gay men. Lesbians are 'doubly invisible'. Stratford claims that gay women are portrayed in the press in one of two ways: either as 'failures' (Julie Goodyear, from *Coronation Street*), or as part of a scandal trying to 'out' women (Whitney Houston). The term lesbian is also used as a smear in an attempt to discredit women. This applied, in particular, to media coverage of the Greenham Common Peace Campaigns and to the campaigns inaugurated by the Greater London Council during the 1980s[17].

The media show more interest in women who conform to sexual stereotypes, and who are involved in 'sexual' stories. The tabloids (and some of the broadsheets) show an enduring interest in rape cases. The coverage of rape has twin appeal for the tabloids. It deals with sex and with violence, both of which sell papers. The tabloids, moreover, slant their stories in line with broader cultural values. It has been argued that the dominant context is that of 'male sexual fantasy'. The *News of the World* is said to treat rape as another way of depicting women as sexual objects[18]. The coverage of the motives and frame of mind of those accused of rape also create distortions. In

---

[17] Stratford, 'Women and the Press', pp133-135.
[18] Edgar, 'Objectivity, bias and truth', p122.

particular, accounts sometimes include statements about the sexual frustration of the offender and refer to his 'natural' sexual drives. This fails to take into account other motives in committing rape[19]. Downing has argued that tabloids often explain away rape as a result of too much alcohol or unbearable sexual frustration, and that this serves to instil fear into women, perpetuate their oppression and fuel male fantasies of sexual conquest. These stories lose their true force by featuring alongside sexually provocative images of women[20].

Those who challenge such images find it particularly difficult to attract sympathetic media attention. Angela Neustatter, in her book *Hyenas in Petticoats,* illustrates the selective way in which feminism and the women's movement have been represented in the media. Her account begins with the feminist disruption of the Miss World Contest in 1970, where women stormed the stage blowing whistles, turning football rattles, and carrying placards containing such phrases as Mis-Judged (calling for an end to beauty contests), Mis-Conception (calling for free contraception) and Mis-Placed (demanding free abortion). The *Daily Express* responded by claiming that this 'trouble' was 'caused by women'. These women were, moreover, compared unfavourably to the contestants, who were still referred to as 'girls'. Bob Hope, the host in 1970, said that anyone '... who would want to try to break up an affair as wonderful as this, they got to be on some kind of dope'[21]. The protesters were arrested and charged with disturbing the peace. In court, they conducted their own defence and claimed that the police had no right to give evidence because they were men. This demonstration and the trial that followed forced the press to address 'women's issues', but the women's movement remained convinced that the press was tied to the male establishment. At the National Women's Liberation Conference

---

[19] Edgar, 'Objectivity, bias and truth', p123.
[20] J. Downing, *The Media Machine*, Pluto: London, 1980, p126.
[21] A. Neustatter, *Hyenas in Petticoats*, Penguin: Harmondsworth, 1989 (1990 edition), p23.

in February 1971, it was argued that the press was `... part of a conspiracy, part male, part capitalist, for the oppression of women'[22].

The women's movement has had to fight continually against the establishment's tendency to view women primarily in physical terms. The tabloid press, in particular, has regarded women in this way. The extent of this was shown in an article by Donald Zec (a columnist in the *Daily Mirror*) on Germaine Greer, a lecturer at Warwick University and author of the feminist classic *Female Eunuch*. Instead of looking at Greer's ideas, Zec concentrated upon her lively character and physical appearance, claiming that she had the `... profile of Garbo and the rump of a show jumper'[23]. The tabloids continue to typecast feminism and the women's movement in this way and have created a short-hand vocabulary to describe feminists. This includes terms like butch, dungaree-clad, crop-headed and bovver girls[24].

It is clear that the media have been more receptive towards (and active in the promotion of) so-called `post-feminism'. The post-feminist is presented as somebody who has no need for the excesses of feminism; one who is successful in her working life, whilst retaining feminine qualities. The post-feminist can be seen, however, as one who has learnt to comply and live according to the rules laid down by men. Neustatter is adamant that there are `... women who don't want to have to achieve success by playing the male game, dressing according to a male construct and denying the validity of feminism'[25]. Many feminists feel frustrated at the media's success in typecasting and belittling their work and ideas. The media remain preoccupied with the image of bra-burning and `... no woman who dares to suggest that women should have a fairer deal from society has ever been allowed to forget that myth'[26]. The media tend to portray feminists in terms of their sometimes outrageous stunts, and

---

[22] Mary Holland cited in Neustatter, *Hyenas in Petticoats,* pp26-28.

[23] Donald Zec cited in Neustatter, *Hyenas in Petticoats,*. p31.

[24] Neustatter, *Hyenas in Petticoats,* p145.

[25] Neustatter, *Hyenas in* Petticoats, p152.

[26] *Is this your life ?*, cited in M. Merck, `Sexism in the Media', p103.

generally show very little respect for feminist perspectives on economic, social and political issues.

Until fairly recently, magazines designed specifically for women have done relatively little to challenge patriarchal views. It has been argued that women's magazines in the post-war period focused upon two main issues. Women were seen as housewives and/or mothers, and as having an interest in personal relationships. Magazines pushed their own ideas of femininity, and were keen to stress that men and women have different but complementary roles[27]. A study of women's magazines during the 1960s and 1970s looked at the cover photos, and the messages they conveyed. There were two main recurrent images: the `chocolate box' face (smiling, warm and `blandly pleasing') and the `invitational' face (with only a hint of a smile, mischievous and with sexual potential). The pictures were of women in their twenties. There was a notable absence of anybody over forty[28].

During the 1970s, feminist magazines and traditional women's magazines were aimed at two different markets. During the 1980s and 1990s, however, some feminist publications moved into the mainstream market. Instead of looking purely at feminist issues, they attempted to attract a broader audience. Some women's magazines have tried to combine feminist issues with glamour. This has hit traditional feminist magazines like *Ms* quite badly. *Ms* has been operating without advertising revenue since 1990, because its editors claimed that make-up and clothes advertisers demanded more sympathetic stories to accompany their products. *Ms* remains committed to hard hitting feminist issues, but has been criticised by the new wave of feminist publications for being too serious, too angry and not enough fun[29]. *Cosmopolitan* became one of the leading magazines for women. It is thought to embrace a form of `aspirational feminism', which emphasises competitiveness, individual success, self-assertion and sexual liberation. Although

[27] A. Tolson, *Mediations*, Arnold: London, 1996, p155.
[28] Downing, *The Media Machine*, p132.
[29] T. Mack, `Women: Did you Ms. me ?', *Guardian*, 30.03.1999.

Cosmopolitan is by no means homophobic, this liberation is still couched within a broadly heterosexual framework and is concerned with overcoming inhibitions[30]. In order to gain a broader audience, the feminist message is usually diluted and made more acceptable to mainstream society.

It is recognised by many feminists that the patriarchal establishment censors women's views far more than those expressed by men. According to Sigrid Nielson, censorship `... isolates; it makes us value ignorance and limits our ability to think independently; it strikes at the basis of all liberation movements, the belief in the power of shared experience to improve life'[31]. Through their possession of economic and social power, men censor on their own behalf, and reinforce the oppression of women by allowing women to be `falsely labelled' as `... passive, available, subservient, willing objects'[32]. In judging where censorship should be used, some feminists employ the criteria of human rights. Liz Kelly, for example, claims that it is important to distinguish between those views that are `progressive' and those that are `oppressive'. This argument allows for the censorship of views that are oppressive and an affront to human rights[33].

Susan Mendus believes that racist and sexist literature should be restricted. This means going beyond the liberal defence of freedom of speech. Mendus claims that the value of free speech lies in its contribution to mutual understanding, but that this mutual understanding has to be created. In her view, the truth will not emerge through the free exchange of ideas. It is not necessary to defend free speech on the grounds that it contributes towards individual development. Instead of viewing the issue in terms of individual rights, she attempts to see it in terms of rights of social

[30] Tolson, *Mediations*, p154 and p158.
[31] S. Neilson, `Books for Bad Women: A Feminist Looks at Censorship', p25 in G. Chester and J. Dickey (eds), *Feminism and Censorship: The Current Debate*, Prism Press: Dorset, 1988, pp17-25.
[32] A. Blue, `Censorship - An Analysis', p105 in Chester and Dickey (eds), *Feminism and Censorship*, pp52-61.
[33] L. Kelley, `The US Ordinances: Censorship or Radical Law Reform', p59 in Chester and Dickey (eds), *Feminism and Censorship*, pp52-61.

groups. Speech is important not only as a means of self expression for the individual, but also as a means of communication. There should be free speech, therefore, when it assists in communication between people. Speech which aims to destroy this communication or hinder mutual understanding does not deserve such protection[34].

Some sections of the media actively campaign against the sexist portrayal of women in the media. The Campaign for Press and Broadcasting Freedom, for example, believe that the media have broad social responsibilities and that there should be restrictions upon racist literature and sexism in the media[35]. The National Union of Journalists also have guidelines against sexism in the media. These include changing the vocabulary we use (chair instead of chairman) and broadening the scope of covering women in the news. It is important to realise that women are also involved in politics and economics, and that men are involved in issues concerning relationships and the family[36].

The media have concentrated for too long upon the activities of men. The tabloids in particular show relatively little interest in women unless they are performing fairly well defined gender roles. Women often feature in the popular press as mothers, girlfriends or mistresses, but rarely in their own right. Women who do not fall into such categories are marginalised and sometimes attacked for not being 'real women'. This limited view of women makes as much sense as seeing men only as fathers, boyfriends or studs. Some of the media seem to have difficulty dealing with women unless they display traditional 'feminine' characteristics. Employing such a narrow definition of what constitutes a 'real woman' excludes many women from media coverage, and makes it virtually impossible for the media to accommodate the various characteristics of women and the various roles they perform.

---

[34] S. Mendus, 'The Tigers of Wrath and the Horses of Instruction', in B. Parekh (ed), *Free Speech*, Commission for Racial Equality: London, 1990, pp3-17.
[35] J. Dickey and G. Chester, 'Introduction', pp8-9 in G. Chester and J. Dickey (eds), *Feminism and Censorship*, Prism Press: Dorset, 1988, pp1-10.
[36] Stratford, 'Women and the Press', p136.

Women and Journalism

Women are under-represented in the profession of journalism. Research on the American media has shown that although there was a rapid increase in women joining the administrative side of the media in the early 1970s, the level of recruitment has declined ever since. Women tend to occupy fairly low-level positions, and have found themselves working as the affirmative action officer or supervising other women or ethnic minorities[37]. Flaws have been exposed in the assumption that women journalists are drawn to a different type of news. Although they are often given *softer* news, women journalists tend to have similar interests to their male colleagues and women journalism students have been found to have as much interest in politics as their male classmates. These students did, however, believe that they were unusual and that the majority of women were probably more interested in the traditional issues covered in `women's pages'[38].

Women journalists are often assigned with the task of writing features `for women', and that this has created some problems for the advancement of women as journalists and for the way women are perceived in society. The first `women's page' was written by Jane Cunningham for the *New York Dispatch* in 1859. This set the tone for similar pages. The `woman's page' often conformed to a `male-devised idea of what women want', and concentrated upon beauty, fashion and cooking. This tone was, however, altered by the *Guardian* in Britain. In 1922, the *Manchester Guardian* launched its own women's page. By the 1950s, this had become a centre of political dissent dealing with women's rights and the problems of inequality[39].

---

[37] G. Tuchman, `Women's depiction by the mass media', p13 in H. Baehr and A. Gray (eds), *Turning it on*, Arnold: London, 1996, pp11-15.

[38] Tuchman, `Women's depiction by the mass media', p13.

[39] Neustatter, *Hyenas in Petticoats,* pp139-140.

There are, however, some political problems stemming from the existence of a distinct woman's page. Frances Cairncross was the editor of the women's page in the *Guardian* for three years. She claims that it was an important feature for it ensured that the paper included a continual flow of articles about women, and that these articles were screened by a woman editor. Its drawback lay, however, in the way that the section was expected to maintain a political commitment; not by the editors, but by its writers and its 'most vocal' readers. This created the situation where journalists censored themselves to suit their readership. Yvonne Roberts, who worked as a features editor on the *London Daily News,* points to another flaw. She claims that it creates the problem of ghettoising such important issues as the family and safety on the streets. These issues affect men as well as women. Their inclusion in the women's page, however, gives the impression that they are solely the concern of women[40].

It could be argued that the restriction of women reporters to the softer or peripheral issues is in decline. The 1980s saw the rise of such important women journalists as Veronica Wadley (*Daily Telegraph*), Brigid Callaghan (*The Times*) and Eve Pollard (*Sunday Mirror*). It was a decade, also, when women were given editorial control over the colour supplements. This coincided, however, with changing priorities. Supplements increasingly looked at lifestyle, homemaking and fitness issues. These supplements targeted, in a very real way, affluent career women and did little to broaden the range of 'women's issues'[41].

Dawn Alford, of the *Mirror*, has criticised the way that women reporters are treated by the profession. Alford broke the story that Jack Straw's son was selling drugs, and became the subject of sexist jibes. Instead of dealing with the story on face value, some columnists and rival journalists accused her of using her 'feminine charms' to entrap William Straw. Alford was described as 'a cross between Mata Hari and a black widow spider'. Other women reporters (Jan Jacques, Nadia Cohen and Louise Oswald) were likewise

---

[40] Neustatter, *Hyenas in Petticoats,* pp141-146.
[41] Neustatter, *Hyenas in Petticoats,* p148.

attacked for practising what has become known as 'honeypot journalism'. Louise Oswald, who wrote a damning expose of Lawrence Dallaglio (the England Rugby captain), was accused by the *Telegraph* of flaunting her charms, by the *Mail* of perpetrating a 'classic honeypot', and by the *Standard* of behaving like a prostitute. Alford claims that these reactions show that 'sexism still exists in a few male-dominated newsrooms and in the narrow minded views of some obscure columnists', and that it should be noted that women reporters deserve respect for the work they do rather than being evaluated according to their looks. The sexism of the media is illustrated by the way that male investigative journalists would be unlikely to provoke a headline like 'Exclusive: The bearded beauty who brought them down. Should these 30-40 year old men be stopped from using their masculine charms ?'[42].

In broadcasting, women have encountered other barriers to autonomy and respect. According to Patricia Holland, women news-readers have to adopt a 'universal voice', defined by masculine language. They are expected to abandon their perspective as women, yet have their physical appearance manufactured in fine detail. They have to appear different from men and, in recent years, in accordance with the image of 'post-feminist' businesswomen[43]. Kirsty Wark, who recently signed a new £600,000 contract with the BBC for presenting programmes including *Newsnight*, is one of the most influential journalists in Britain, yet still has to endure '... unreconstructed sexism about her looks, legs, clothes, super-mum status, her packed lunches for the kids, her ordinariness in still being able to make a cup of tea'[44]. She describes herself as a natural feminist, and finds it strange that some women reject the feminist label. She complains that she is always asked about how she can juggle family and work. She believes that it is an inappropriate question because such things are a lot easier for those with money,

---

[42] D. Alford, 'Would you care if I had a beard ?', *Guardian,* 31.05.1999.

[43] Holland, 'When a woman reads the news', pp198-199.

[44] D. Fraser, 'Power Players', *Guardian,* 8.02.1999.

and something approaching a nightmare for single parents on benefits or in poorly paid work[45].

Women in radio encounter less barriers to a successful career. Liesbet van Zoonen argues that women are more likely to be employed in low-status media than in those at the cutting edge of technology. In the west, this is shown by a high percentage of women in radio and in local news services. Men dominate the high prestige media. The media tend to have high expectations of the women they employ. These extend beyond mere professionalism to matters of personal appearance and ideals of femininity[46]. Although women tend to have more success in finding work in radio than they do in TV, women find that they are not given jobs as DJs (who dominate radio presentation). Male DJs and 'programme controllers' have argued that this is because relatively few women are interested in becoming DJs, women lack the technical expertise necessary to function well in the job, and that the radio audience prefers to hear the voice of a man. It has been argued that these responses are similar to 'new racist' discourse. They deny that there is any prejudice on their part, and attribute the lack of women DJs to the limitations of women and to the prejudices of the radio audience[47].

Women have often found it difficult to disrupt patriarchal control of the media and to change the images of women from inside the media itself. The media is male dominated, and this has placed institutional and professional constraints upon the activities of women. Some scholars doubt the wisdom of attempting to reform from within, for such interventions can only result in the watering down of feminist aims and the re-enforcement of '... simpler and more acceptable ideas already existing in the dominant culture'[48]. Some women, therefore, prefer to remain outside mainstream media and in control of their own activities.

---

[45] K. Wark cited in Fraser, 'Power Players'.
[46] Liesbet van Zoonen in J. Watson, *Media Communication*, pp169-170.
[47] R. Gill, 'Ideology, gender and popular radio', in Baehr and Gray (eds), *Turning it on*, pp211-217.
[48] T. de Lauretis (1987) cited in Baehr and Gray, *Turning it on*, p166. See also p165.

There is a chilling lesson to be learned from the history of *Broadside*; a feminist inspired and women led production company which gained commissions for two series of current affairs programmes from the new Channel 4 between 1982-1983. Jeremy Issacs, the chief executive of Channel 4, had given the commissions to *Broadside* in the hope of gaining a `woman's angle' on current affairs. *Broadside* aimed to produce programmes that reflected feminist views rather than aspire to provide impartial accounts. It was not its intention to preach to the converted, but to make programmes as accessible and as interesting as possible. Channel 4, however, demanded that *Broadside* appoint a senior editor and that the company operated using a clear chain of command. This created serious problems for *Broadside*, which had been set up with a non-hierarchical structure. The imposed structure undermined collective effort, created dissatisfaction and tensions within the company, and subverted its feminist aims. *Broadside* did much to `... challenge the conventions of an industry which had hampered women's progress yet, by working in that industry, it internalised many of its professional practices and aspirations'[49]

Just as women are marginalised in the news, so women journalists are often assigned to cover `women's issues' and side-tracked from covering broader economic and political news. Many women journalists have found that they are evaluated too often according to their physical attributes, and that they are expected to conform to the expectations of their male colleagues. Far more thought is dedicated to the clothes and image of women presenters than to appearance of their male counterparts. These expectations place constraints upon women journalists, and effectively limit the challenge they can make to media stereotypes of women.

---

[49] H. Baehr and A. Spindler-Brown, `Firing a Broadside: A Feminist intervention into mainstream TV', in Baehr and Gray (eds), *Turning it on*, pp183-189.

Conclusion

Sexism is a form of prejudice and discrimination, which is incompatible with the ideals of liberal democracy. Democracy cannot work effectively if it subordinates fifty percent of the population. Feminist writers have pointed out that gender roles are socially determined and are reinforced through such institutions as the family, the education system and the media. The media perpetuate sexism by excluding women from serious news, by portraying women in a limited range of roles, by defining women in terms of their relations with men, and by placing far too much emphasis upon their physical attributes and appearance. Women who fight against such stereotypes are often labelled as 'trouble makers' and even as 'failures'. Stereotypical images and views of women reinforce discrimination in society and do little to capture the diversity of modern life. Failure to correct such prejudicial coverage reflects badly upon the media.

7. Terrorism

Terrorism involves the use of violence or the threat of violence to force radical change. The term is often used in a pejorative way. Many so-called terrorists may well refer to themselves as freedom fighters, fighting a just war against an unrepresentative government or foreign power. The media are important tool for modern terrorist groups. Publicity is needed to maximise the psychological impact of terrorism; it can weaken the enemy, create fear, enlist support and strengthen the resolve of the terrorist group. In order to become newsworthy, terrorists engage in spectacular and dangerous stunts. Explosions attract attention. Terrorist groups have over time become skilful at dealing with the media. They issue press releases, take part in news conferences and provide journalists with necessary background information[1]. Modern states often have to deal with a variety of terrorist groups. Some will be fighting international wars, while others are concerned primarily with national liberation from supposed foreign domination. The Irish Republican Army (IRA) fall into the latter category. It does not attempt to convert the world to Irish Catholicism, but to remedy an ancient political evil; the British partition and occupation of Northern Ireland.

An introduction to Irish politics

Ireland was conquered by Tudor monarchs in the sixteenth century, but the Irish refused to become loyal to their Protestant rulers. This led the British colonisation of Ireland with Scottish and English settlers. In the seventeenth century, the British re-conquered Ireland twice. These invasions were orchestrated by Cromwell and William of Orange respectively. Throughout the eighteenth century, the Protestants increased their power and administered the affairs of the country from its own parliament in Dublin. The power of the

---

[1] See McNair, *An Introduction to Political Communication*, pp153-155.

Protestants relied upon the exclusion of Catholics from the franchise. This was rectified, to some extent, by the Catholic Relief Act of 1793 which gave Catholics the right to vote, but not the right to sit in parliament. In 1791, the United Irishmen was formed to advance the cause of Catholic emancipation. Its leader, Wolfe Tone, claimed that the aim of the organisation was to `... break the connection with England, the never-failing source of all our political evils, and to assert the independence of my country'[2]. In 1798, the United Irishmen led a rebellion. Although the rebellion was crushed, it did frighten the British government. In the interests of geo-political security, William Pitt responded with the Act of Union of 1801 which integrated the Irish Parliament with Westminster.

Throughout the nineteenth century, Irish nationalists pushed for an end to the union and for the independence of Ireland. One of the most important of the Irish nationalist movements was the Irish Republican Brotherhood, known also as the Fenians. During the 1860s and 1870s, the Fenians were engaged in terrorist activity in mainland Britain. This activity effectively forced the British government to look into the prospects for Irish home rule. The first home rule bill was placed before parliament by Gladstone in 1886. This bill called for an independent Irish executive responsible to an Irish parliament, though Westminster would maintain control over defense, foreign affairs and would still have some control over Irish economic policy. This rather modest bill was defeated by 343 to 313 votes, split the Liberal Party and brought down the government. When Gladstone resumed power, he continued to pledge his support for home rule. His bill of 1893 was passed in the House of Commons, but rejected by the Lords. Gladstone resigned in response, and the Conservative Unionist Party resumed power. This bill, however, had some important repercussions. Firstly, it prompted the Irish Unionists to organise themselves militarily so that they could resist home rule. Secondly, it radicalised the Irish nationalists. Many nationalists believed that constitutional tactics were useless and formed Sinn Fein which

---

[2] B. O'Leary and J. McGarry, *The Politics of Antagonism*, The Athlone Press: London, 1993, p71.

recommended direct action rather than political participation. Finally, it encouraged the British government to reform conditions in Ireland so as to reduce the appeal of nationalism. One of the most important reforms was the Wyndham Act of 1903 which gave Irish tenant farmers the right to buy their land.

The cause of home rule was revived again in 1910. The liberal government of 1906 promised to look into home rule, but this was not given precedence until the Irish Party gained seats in the General Election of 1910. Although the Liberals won the election, their majority depended upon the support of the Irish Party. In April 1912, the third home rule bill was placed before parliament. This bill would allow for some powers to be given to an Irish parliament. The Conservatives, who were dominant in the north of Ireland, rejected this move and organised a petition demanding that Ulster be excluded from the home rule legislation. The home rule bill was passed through the commons twice in 1913, and vetoed on both occasions by the House of Lords. In June 1914, the government agreed to the north opting out. The onset of the First World War, however, meant that this legislation was suspended until the end of the war. Nationalists continued to push for home rule. In April 1916, the Easter rising was suppressed and its leaders executed. Sinn Fein benefited from an upsurge in nationalism. In December 1918, Sinn Fein won 73 of the 105 Irish seats at Westminster, but refused to attend. Instead, Sinn Fein decided to set up its own parliament in Dublin. This allowed the Ulster Unionists to negotiate more preferable terms with the British government for the exclusion of Ulster from home rule.

In 1920, the government issued the fourth home rule bill (The Government of Ireland Act). This called for two parliaments in Ireland; one in Belfast, the other in Dublin. This failed to gain the support of Sinn Fein and contributed towards the war of independence between 1920-1921. The British government sought an agreement with Sinn Fein and secured the Anglo-Irish Treaty in December 1921. This treaty stated that southern Ireland would be independent and northern Ireland would have dominion status under the crown. This would not necessarily be a permanent partition[3].

The motives behind the partitioning of Ireland are, of course, the subject of controversy. From a nationalist perspective, the partition was artificial. Britain is said to have been motivated by imperial sentiments. Having lost the bulk of Ireland, it still wanted to exert influence in the north. Britain thus manipulated religious differences in the hope of justifying its presence. The moderate perspective, on the other hand, attributes the partition to religious differences rather than to British intervention. This perspective claims that it was the Irish who partitioned Ireland and that violence in Ireland stems from irreconcilable differences[4].

The British government delegated power to a regional parliament held at Stormont, Belfast. This parliament was dominated by the Unionists until 1972. The Catholics were effectively excluded from power by gerrymandering and by official discrimination. Electoral boundaries were re-drawn to ensure a Protestant majority. There was also large scale discrimination in employment. In Derry, for example, 80% of council employees were Protestant and there were no Catholic heads of department. The implications of such discrimination were noted in the 1969 Cameron Report. This report stated that grievances in Northern Ireland had stemmed from its single party government. It argued that the opposition had been excluded from any likelihood of power and that this had led to a decline in responsibility. The dominant party was seen as unshakeable. This made it complacent and unwilling to change. The Catholic community thus felt alienated from Stormont and it was estimated that 50 % of Catholics in Northern Ireland wanted to re-unify with the south[5].

Between 1968 and 1972, violence increased in opposition to Stormont. This situation became increasingly unstable. In the

[3] O' Leary and McGarry, *The Politics of Antagonism*, pp84-101.
[4] A. Seldon, 'Northern Ireland', p552 in B. Jones et al, *Politics UK*, Philip Allan: Hemel Hempstead, 1991, pp550-565.
[5] P.J. Madgwick, D. Steeds and L. Williams, *Britain since 1945*, Hutchinson: London, 1982, pp328-329.

summer of 1969, riots took place in Belfast and in Londonderry. This urged the Stormont government to request military assistance from Britain. The Stormont government maintained control over the police, but the British army took its orders from London. In return for military assistance, Stormont promised to tackle some of the grievances of the Catholic community; but little was done. The division between the communities in Northern Ireland were widened, and by 1970 both the Catholics and the Protestants were armed. Civil rights movements, like Bernadette Devlin's 'People's Democracy', developed along the same lines as the American civil rights movements. This group relied upon demonstrations rather than violence and called for the unity of the working class across religious divisions. The police, however, suppressed its activities and thus fuelled discontent. This reached a peak in January 1972 with so called 'Bloody Sunday' when the police shot 13 civilians during a civil rights march. The repercussions were extensive. Devlin assaulted the home secretary on the floor of the House of Commons, and 6 soldiers were killed in Aldershot. In response, the British government suspended Stormont and introduced direct rule[6].

When Britain assumed control over Northern Ireland, it was intended only as a temporary measure. Within a year, William Whitelaw had outlined a plan for power sharing in Northern Ireland. There was to be a joint executive (nationalist and unionist) and an assembly elected upon the basis of proportional representation. This, it was hoped, would create a permanent coalition between the two communities. In addition, there was to be a 'council of Ireland', consisting of delegates from the north and south. This council was intended to assist in relations between the two halves of Ireland, and to act as a forum for common issues. In a referendum held in Northern Ireland in 1973, 57 % voted in favour of staying in the UK. This referendum was, however, boycotted by all Catholic parties. In December 1973, Dublin accepted that any change in the status of Northern Ireland depended upon the support of the majority in

---

[6] Madgwick, Steeds and Williams, *Britain since 1945*, p330 and Seldon, 'Northern Ireland', pp553-556.

Northern Ireland. The Loyalists, who were against such provisos, led a general strike against the government in Northern Ireland and brought down the power sharing executive[7].

The politics of Northern Ireland are complicated by religious divisions, and by questions of legitimacy. For many of the nationalist movements, British involvement in Irish politics lacks legitimacy and true authority. The British government have been able to exert power and influence, but nationalists tend to argue that the British have no right to this influence. Nationalists have thus rejected British compromises, and demanded that Britain withdraw from Ireland and leave the Irish to run their own country. Nationalists have argued that unless the British withdraw voluntarily, they will be forced out with violence. For many nationalists, the Irish are at war with the British.

Northern Ireland and the Media: 1968-1988

Northern Ireland became an issue for the British media in 1968. Many in the media had very little knowledge of the background to Irish politics, and slipped into viewing the Catholic civil rights marches as simply Irish versions of civil rights protests in continental Europe and in the United States. In the absence of any further understanding, the media deferred to the position of the British government. When British troops entered Northern Ireland, the press in particular emphasised how the troops were welcomed by the Catholic community. It ignored the problems that the Catholic community had encountered, and blamed a minority of nationalists for stirring up trouble against the British forces. Martin Bell recalls that he was instructed to conceal the widespread violence directed at Catholics. Catholics were being burned out of their homes and attacked in the streets by unionist groups. News coverage showed these attacks but neglected to mention that the victims were Catholic. It was deemed to be too inflammatory[8].

---

[7]   Madgwick, Steeds and Williams, *Britain since 1945*, pp330-331, and Seldon, 'Northern Ireland', pp553-557.
[8]   *The Information War*, BBC2, 16.08.1994.

Throughout the 1970s, the British media reproduced information fed to them by army intelligence. The British media concealed the truth about 'Bloody Sunday' (January 1972). The confusion and chaos which led to the deaths of 13 civil rights marchers was brushed aside in favour of the army's interpretation. Colin Wallace, of the Army Press Office, informed the media that a number of those who had been killed had direct terrorist links. This story was untrue. The Army Press Office continued to exert a heavy influence over media coverage, and was instrumental in planting deliberately false information in its war against terrorism. The army were unable to conduct body searches on women, and suspected that the IRA was using women to smuggle its explosives. Wallace responded with his 'exploding underwear' story which claimed that women smuggling explosives in their underwear were likely to trigger explosions because their underwear generated static electricity. He also planted a story that abandoned houses were being used for black magic. The Army Press Office went so far as to kit out houses with black magic symbols, candles and chicken blood so as to provide a visual record for the press. This was spun so as to create suspicion in the community towards 'outsiders' and to deprive the IRA of possible hideouts[9].

Although many of these stories were untrue, they were at least imaginative and entertaining. Jim Campbell of *Sunday World* claimed that the entertainment value of these stories attracted the press, even though the press knew that the stories were blatant propaganda. Charles Moore of the *Sunday Telegraph* claimed that the Army Press Office was a convenience, for it meant that individual journalists did not have to think their own way through the issues. Moore describes this as a 'characteristically British way' of dealing with problems, and that the media were guilty of 'collective mental laziness'[10]. The IRA responded by attempting to use the media to publicise its own activities, and links grew between the IRA and some sections of the media.

---

[9] Jim Campbell and Colin Wallace interviewed in *The Information War*.

[10] Charles Moore interviewed in *The Information War*.

It was apparent by 1979 that Mrs. Thatcher was unhappy with media coverage of terrorism. On the eve of the 1979 General Election, the Irish National Liberation Army (a Marxist faction which had recently withdrawn from the IRA) assassinated Mrs. Thatcher's friend and advisor Airey Neave. Within a few weeks, the BBC released an interview with a member from the INLA. Mrs. Thatcher felt contempt for the journalist responsible for this interview. Lady Neave (Airey Neave's widow), was not warned before the programme appeared. She wrote a letter of protest which was published in the *Daily Telegraph* and was joined by many Conservative MPs. Mrs. Thatcher considered taking action against the BBC under the Prevention of Terrorism Act of 1976. On this occasion, no formal action was taken; but it did serve as a warning to the media[11].

Within three months, the BBC was involved in another controversy over its handling of Ireland. The *Panorama* team were told that they would find something of interest if they visited the small republican village of Carrickmore. Upon arriving, they found that the village was being patrolled by armed IRA members. Before this material could be broadcast, the *Financial Times* broke the story about the experiences of the journalists. Bernard Ingham, Mrs. Thatcher's Press Secretary, apparently 'exploded on the spot' when he read of their exploits. In his view, the media should not be in the business of publicising the activities of terrorist groups. Mrs. Thatcher once again attacked the BBC, and in May 1980 the attorney-general Sir Michael Havers told the House of Commons that the BBC were in breach of the Prevention of Terrorism Act; it had, after all, been in contact with terrorists and had failed to report this to the police. The BBC responded by temporarily suspending Roger Bolton, the editor of *Panorama*, and by suppressing all footage of Carrickmore. Bolton was incensed. The BBC, he argued, must maintain its independence from the government[12].

---

[11] G. Edgerton, 'Quelling the Oxygen of Publicity', pp 116-118 *Journal of Popular Culture*, Volume 30, Summer 1996, pp115-131.

[12] Edgerton, 'Quelling the Oxygen of Publicity', pp118-119 and *Auntie: The Inside Story of the BBC : Part 4*, BBC1, 18.11.1997

Throughout its first term of office, the Thatcher government prompted the BBC and ITV to censor themselves over their handling of terrorist issues. It was implied that this would avoid the need for overt government censorship. During the period 1979-1983, thirteen TV programmes were suppressed for political reasons[13]. By 1985, Mrs. Thatcher's attitude became more confrontational. When the American media covered the TWA hijacking in Beirut, Mrs. Thatcher claimed that media coverage provided the terrorists with the 'oxygen of publicity' and that news organisations should place their own voluntary ban on reporting terrorist activity[14].

Within two weeks the British government was involved in overt censorship of delicate material. The controversy arose over the proposed broadcast of a programme entitled *At the Edge of the Union* which had been produced by the BBC as part of the *Real Lives* series. This programme was thought to show Martin McGuinness (a leading member of Sinn Fein and a suspected member of the IRA) in a too favourable light. The initial filming of the programme had taken place during a relatively quite time in the Irish conflict. During the editing stage, however, the situation changed. Mrs. Thatcher was outraged when during a trip to America she was told by a journalist that the BBC intended to broadcast the *Real Lives* programme. Leon Brittan (the Home Secretary) asked the BBC to suppress the programme; claiming that it was not desirable for the BBC to give coverage to those who use murder as a political weapon. The board of governors agreed to do so, creating a serious rift between itself and the Director General Alistair Milne and provoking a one day protest strike by journalists at the BBC and the ITV. The programme was eventually broadcast in a revised form in October 1986. Mrs. Thatcher, however, denied that she had been involved in any direct censorship of the media[15].

---

[13] Edgerton, 'Quelling the Oxygen of Publicity' p121.
[14] Edgerton, 'Quelling the Oxygen of Publicity', p115.
[15] Edgerton, 'Quelling the Oxygen of Publicity', p122 and *Auntie: The Inside Story of the BBC, Part 4*, and *The Information War*.

The final controversy came in 1988 with the IBA's programme *Death on the Rock*. This programme revealed that members of the British SAS had executed three unarmed members of the IRA in Gibraltar. Sir Geoffrey Howe, the Foreign Secretary, telephoned Lord Thomson at the IBA and attempted to persuade him to postpone the programme. Thomson refused and the government responded by launching an investigation into the programme's production team. Six months later, a formal ban on terrorist broadcasts was introduced. This effectively ended the government's reliance upon the media deferring to the British interpretation and censoring themselves. According to the government, the media had gone too far in considering the nationalist agenda and had failed to understand the importance of supporting the establishment.

The Broadcast ban

In October 1988, the British Home Secretary (Douglas Hurd) banned broadcasts by any of the paramilitary organisations in Northern Ireland, including Sinn Fein and the IRA. Mrs. Thatcher justified it by claiming that in war, some civil liberties must be suspended. She believed that the British government was at war with the IRA, and that placing restrictions upon freedom of expression was therefore legitimate. It was hoped that such a ban would deprive the terrorist groups (and those who support them) of the publicity they need to survive[16]. The broadcast ban forbade the media broadcasting 'any words spoken' by people representing or attempting to gain support for specific organisations including the IRA, INLA, Sinn Fein, Republican Sinn Fein and the Ulster Defence Association[17].

The broadcast ban did not dissuade journalists from delving into the politics of Northern Ireland. Peter Taylor, who made *Inside Story:*

---

[16]   P. Gilbert, 'The Oxygen of Publicity: Terrorism and Reporting Restrictions', in A. Belsey and R. Chadwick (eds), *Ethical Issues in Journalism and the Media*, Routledge: London, 1992, pp137-153, and Edgerton, 'Quelling the Oxygen of Publicity'.

[17]   Edgerton, 'Quelling the Oxygen of Publicity', p123, and Petley, 'The Regulation of Media Content', p149.

Enemies Within (1990) clamed that he ignored the restrictions when making the programme, and left others to determine how the restrictions were to be applied. He was allowed access to nationalist and loyalist terrorists in the Maze Prison. The vast majority of these interviews remained in the final cut; with one notable exception. The BBC imposed the broadcast ban on a section where a spokesperson for the IRA complained about the size of the sausage rolls to the prison catering staff. The cut had to be made because he was speaking in an official capacity, rather than expressing personal views[18].

The broadcast ban has been justified in the interests of security. It has been argued that the success of military campaigns against terrorism rely upon an element of surprise, and that this can justify limiting information available to non-military personnel. Gilbert believes, however, that this is a smokescreen since counter-terrorist operations are not carried out like wars. It also ignores the fact that people in `war zones' need information so that they can protect themselves[19] . Counter-terrorism relies upon preserving morale and eroding the enemy's will to continue. This can be achieved, to some extent, by giving the impression that life is going on as normal and that the national government and security forces remain in control. Such messages serve to conceal both the gains made by terrorist groups and the use made of suspect tactics by the state[20].

Gilbert claims that restricting information can cause considerable harm to those living in areas of conflict. Ordinary citizens may be subject to state coercion, and it serves to distort our idea of the public good. By concealing information, the government strengthens its own position to determine and judge the nature of the `public good'. According to Gilbert, the temptation to `... substitute the sectional interest of a particular government for that of the public at large is too strong when the success of the policy is not open to public scrutiny'[21].

---

[18] Peter Taylor interviewed in *The Information War*.
[19] Gilbert, `The Oxygen of Publicity', pp137-139.
[20] Gilbert, `The Oxygen of Publicity', p139.
[21] Gilbert, `The Oxygen of Publicity', p140.

The main problem is that the state and terrorist groups will have different interpretations of the national interest. This is particularly the case where `... the official State view of what constitutes a nation is under challenge from the terrorists'[22].

The `democratic argument' claims that placing restrictions upon those who side-step the democratic process does in no way pose a threat to democracy. A pure democratic argument might state that people need access to a wide range of information and opinion to judge a government and to go beyond the government's interpretation of events. It might be argued that terrorists are not contending for political power through the democratic process; they should therefore not be given the right to freedom of expression. Gilbert denies the validity of this argument, and states that the public needs to know the truth[23].

Terrorist groups can also be regarded as `illegitimate' and therefore unworthy of freedom of expression. It has been argued that terrorism is by nature wrong given that it relies upon violence rather than debate to solve political problems. What this fails to take into account is that terrorism is often associated with national liberation movements. These groups will tend to regard the governing state as illegitimate. The state may wish to justify its actions by saying that regardless of the wishes of the people in a given territory, the state has power because of history. This is known as the `involuntarist' argument. The opposing `voluntarist' position states that the opinions of members of the community about the nature of their community must be heard, for the legitimacy of government depends upon the `popular will'[24].

Gilbert claims that the broadcast ban is an act of political suppression. It excludes certain groups from participating in political debate. They can continue to express their views, but these views will not be transmitted in their original form. By suppressing the voices of those who support terrorist activity, the ban effectively `... abstracts

---

[22] Gilbert, `The Oxygen of Publicity', p140.
[23] Gilbert, `The Oxygen of Publicity', pp142-143.
[24] Gilbert, `The Oxygen of Publicity', pp144-147.

the views they hold from their lives and actions as individuals participating in a common life and able to enter a dialogue with others'[25]. This suppression of dissident voices creates the illusion that there is a common will, and serves to de-moralise the dissidents. These dissidents are, in many ways, blamed for excluding themselves from the political community[26].

The broadcast ban has been criticised by politicians and journalists in Britain, and by the international community. Paddy Ashdown of the Liberal Democrats said `... you cannot defeat terrorism by destroying our liberties. This action is potentially dangerous, likely unworkable, and almost certainly ineffective'[27]. Journalists in Britain were likewise outraged. John Birt, the Director-General of the BBC, said that the broadcast ban `... crosses a line that governments in democratic societies should not cross'[28]. A group of journalists challenged the ban through the courts, but lost their case in the High Court, the Appeals Court and in the House of Lords in the period between May 1989 and February 1991. The journalists argued that they had a duty to be impartial and that the ban distorted the truth by suppressing pertinent facts. The ban therefore produced only partial (and biased) accounts of events[29]. The restrictions were hailed as undemocratic, dictatorial and hostile to freedom in both the American and Russian press[30]. The British government had violated our civil liberties.

The Thatcher government believed that its war against the IRA warranted severe restrictions upon freedom of speech. Throughout the 1980s, the media was pressured by the government and was eventually muzzled in its treatment of Sinn Fein and the IRA. It is clear that the Thatcher government had no interest in hearing the case put forward by these groups. Indeed, it was not until the post-

---

[25] Gilbert, `The Oxygen of Publicity', p148.
[26] Gilbert, `The Oxygen of Publicity', pp149-150.
[27] Ashdown cited in Edgerton, `Quelling the Oxygen of Publicity', p123.
[28] Birt cited in Edgerton, `Quelling the Oxygen of Publicity', p126.
[29] Edgerton, `Quelling the Oxygen of Publicity', p125 and Gilbert, `The Oxygen of Publicity', pp141-142.
[30] Edgerton, `Quelling the Oxygen of Publicity', pp124-125.

Thatcher era that this war against the IRA gave way to the 'peace process', and freedom of speech for terrorist groups (and their supporters) was recognised as legitimate once more. The broadcast ban was eventually lifted in September 1994.

Conclusion

The media have played an important role in the British government's campaign against the IRA. Ken Loach argues that there is systemic bias in media coverage of Northern Ireland. Television news in particular does not stray from the British view of the conflict. The news focuses on the disarming of the IRA, but does not expect the Royal Ulster Constabulary to follow suit[31]. The media rarely show any sympathy towards terrorists. Although terrorists can attract media attention, it does not mean that their cause will be covered in any detail and terrorist sources are rarely treated with the same degree of respect as government sources[32]. Failure to look into the reasons for terrorist acts reduces terrorism to mere criminal activity. It is clear that successive British governments have regarded the IRA as criminals and murderers. The British government has taken steps to ensure that this interpretation of the IRA has been reinforced by the media. Much of the media have deferred to the British state and excluded the nationalist perspective. In coercing the media to report the conflict from a British perspective, the British state has undermined the freedom of the media.

---

[31] Ken Loach in *And Finally Part One: The Metropolitan Line*.
[32] McNair, *An Introduction to Political Communication*, pp154-156.

8. War

It is sometimes thought that truth is the `first casualty of war', for national unity is such a precious asset for those nations involved in active warfare. If the population can be convinced that the war is `just', it will be more likely to accept hardship and make the sacrifices that the war demands. This will often involve the state taking an active part in `selling the war' and in limiting the circulation of material thought to be `harmful' to the war effort. The public's `right to know' is often circumvented during times of war. This has been justified by the likes of Peregrine Worsthorne who claims that the public has no interest in the truth if it threatens to harm the war effort. He argues that public prefer to leave the conduct of war to `the authorities' and favour relatively little scrutiny by the media[1].

It is sometimes argued that it is inappropriate to be `objective' during times of war. During the Spanish Civil War, for example, a number of reporters including Ernest Hemingway, George Orwell and Charles Cockburn were fighting with the International Brigades. This undoubtedly influenced their reporting. Herbert Matthews of the *New York Times* said that journalists should write with `honest bias', and should use their hearts as well as their heads[2]. This might involve concealing unpleasant truths from the public. Charles Cockburn believed that reporters had an obligation to what is *right* rather than to what is *true*[3]. Max Hastings of the *Telegraph* claimed during the Falklands War that reporters should assist in the winning of wars, and he admitted that his own coverage of the war identified completely with the interests, feelings and activities of the British forces. There

---

[1]   K. Williams, `Something more important than truth', pp 157-158 in A. Belsey and R. Chadwick (eds), *Ethical Issues in Journalism and the Media*, Routledge: London, 1992, pp154-170.
[2]   Williams, `Something more important than truth', p163.
[3]   Cockburn cited in Williams, `Something more important than the truth', p163.

was enough time to be objective when the war was over[4]. Less than ten years later, he made a similar point when discussing the responsibilities of war correspondents in the Gulf. He claimed that although journalists should remain sceptical of government claims during times of war, he remained `... unconvinced of the case for displaying `objectivity' as between the allies and Saddam, when even the most generous moral assessment of his deeds already in this war suggests that he is an exceptionally evil man'[5]. For Hastings, it is disloyal to give the `enemy' a fair hearing; for such liberal sensibilities can jeopardise the war effort.

The aspiration to produce objective war coverage has also been criticised from a more humanitarian angle. Martin Bell recalls that when he joined the BBC during the 1960s, he accepted and worked in accordance with its tradition of objective journalism. When reporting on wars he looked at the technical aspects of the war rather than the human story. He has since come to believe that it is important to distinguish between right and wrong, and to be an open advocate of the `journalism of attachment'. He argues that the journalist is not and should not be a neutral observer in war. There exists a `dynamic interaction' between the journalist and the event he or she is reporting. It is inappropriate to remain neutral when surrounded by such human misery as is found in war zones. A journalist should be engaged in a `moral enterprise' and make moral judgements[6]. This view is shared by Michael Nicholson who claims that journalists should wear their heart on their sleeves, and get as close as they can to their story rather than remain on the sidelines as an impartial observer. Nicholson, who has been accused of being too personally involved in his stories,

---

[4] Williams, `Something more important than the truth', p156.

[5] M. Hastings, `Saddam and the Media' pp 109-110, in B. Macarthur (ed), *Despatches from the Gulf War*, Bloomsbury: London, 1991, pp109-110.

[6] M. Bell, `The Journalism of Attachment', in M. Kieran (ed), *Media Ethics*, Routledge: London, 1998, pp15-22.

says in response to his critics that `... I don't need advice on how to behave as a human being or a journalist'[7].

What is published during times of war is, however, often monitored, manipulated and controlled by the state. In wars, we are urged to take sides. We are expected to support our own nation, and tolerate any infringements upon our civil liberties. It is argued that such infringements are necessary in order to avoid `giving comfort to the enemy', or posing a threat to our national security. Even the most liberal regimes use some form of censorship during times of war.

Censorship in war

Official censorship has been used in war time throughout the twentieth century. This form of censorship serves a number of functions. In addition to concealing sensitive material from the enemy, it has tended to be used to secure support for the war, to enhance morale, and to cover-up political and military failures. In Britain, for example, the government has imposed official censorship during times of war since the formation of the Press Bureau in 1914. This was replaced by the Ministry of Information during the Second World War. Even in relatively modern times, the government has maintained firm control over the media. The Broadcasting Act of 1981, for example, gave the government direct control over the broadcasting of information; powers it used extensively during the Falklands War of 1982[8].

Individual writers and producers often censor themselves during times of war. They conceal information in the `national interest' or out of loyalty to the national troops. During the First World War, the journalist Philip Gibbs claimed that there was little need for official

---

[7] Michael Nicholson interviewed by Andrew Duncan in `If more reporters showed emotion, TV news wouldn't be losing so many viewers', p10 *Radio Times*, 25.09.1999, pp8-12.

[8] Williams, `Something more important than the truth', pp158-159 and C. Ponting, *Secrecy in Britain*, Blackwell: Oxford, 1990, p29.

censorship for the media censored themselves [9]. Self-censorship was quite common during the Second World War. Many editors of the British press were critical of the Ministry of Information for being too lenient. The press seemed content to abandon objectivity in reporting in favour of bolstering the nation's morale. Direct censorship was fairly minimal because of high levels of self-censorship[10].

The legitimacy of censorship during times of war is open to debate. In an editorial written for *The Independent* during the Gulf war of 1991, it was argued that truth was unavoidably the `first casualty' of war. It claimed that some restrictions upon what is said are justifiable and gave the examples of any military information which would be of value to the enemy, rumours which might endanger military operations or undermine morale, and details of death tolls prior to the next of kin being informed. There were some areas, however, that were less clear. The editorial argued that the media should not be restrained in order to prevent embarrassment to the military or the government of the day. They should not lose their independence and become overtly propagandist. Ministers of a government should always be made accountable for their activities. *The Independent* acknowledged that it was important to ensure that `sensitive material' remained concealed, but argued that `sensitivity and restraint' must be combined with `honesty and courage'[11]. These guidelines suggest that journalists have a duty to support those involved in combat and their families, but that does not mean that there should be no criticism of the war. To say that some information should be censored during wars is by no means the same as saying that the official interpretation of the war should be accepted without question.

It is usually a question of how much and what type of information should be censored during wars. The argument in favour of war time censorship has been put forward by such notable commentators as Sir

---

[9] Philip Gibbs cited in J. Pilger, `The Myth-Makers' p34 in B. Macarthur (ed), *Despatches from the Gulf War*, Bloomsbury: London, 1991, pp33-37.
[10] Williams, `Something more important than truth', 161-163 and p168, Ponting, *Secrecy in Britain,* p 30, Curran, `Press History', p67.
[11] `Journalism and Patriotism', *The Independent*, 18 January 1991 in B. Macarthur (ed), *Despatches from the Gulf War*, pp114-115.

Robin Day. Writing twenty years before the Gulf War, he claimed that television coverage of wars was making it virtually impossible for democracies to wage war. Television coverage of war was so shocking that it ran the risk of `... sapping perhaps the will of that nation to resist the forces of evil or even to safeguard its own freedom'[12]. He claimed that the `... sight of a dead child, a burning home, a dying citizen-soldier - all these may have a much more powerful impact than abstract concepts like `liberty' or `collective security'[13]. It could be argued, however, that concealing the horrors of warfare is an abuse of censorial power. It gives the impression that wars are fought without victims and thus lends legitimacy to wars per se. The Day rationale for restricting coverage of wars has also been criticised for showing contempt for the general public. Writing in the *Sunday Times* in 1991, Robert Harris claimed that general public are perfectly aware that wars are bloody and terrifying. Exposure to images confirming this would not lead to a sudden increase in pacifism. Censorship is far more likely to encourage suspicion towards the government, and contribute towards anti-war feelings[14].

Censorship, even during wars, is not necessarily a good thing. Most commentators and journalists recognise the need for some censorship and restraint to ensure that the lives of troops are not made any more vulnerable. Those who fight wars on our behalf deserve, at the very least, the security necessary for success in military campaigns. This does not mean, however, that the government that sends these troops should be free from scrutiny. Wars are used as political weapons. They are sometimes fought to protect or further vested interests, or to divert attention away from problems `at home'. The press and broadcasting community should be free to explore the motives behind war and question the judgements of our elected representatives.

---

[12]   Robin Day cited in R. Harris, `Don't Shoot the Messenger' p142 in B. Macarthur (ed), *Despatches from the Gulf War*, pp141-142
[13]   Harris, `Don't Shoot the Messenger', p142.
[14]   Harris, `Don't Shoot the Messenger', p142.

Censorship and total wars

Total wars are where the resources of the nation are mobilised for the war effort. They might involve such things as conscription, wartime production quotas, rationing and the curtailment of civil liberties. These wars are directed by governments free from the pressure of General Elections. They involve conquering or being conquered. They are total in the sacrifices they expect the population to make, and in the dire implications of failure. During the twentieth century, the two world wars of 1914-1918 and 1939-1945 fall into this category.

Britain had a system of official censorship during the First World War. Lloyd George, leader of the wartime coalition, was fully aware of the importance of concealing information. He told C.P. Scott, the editor of the *Manchester Guardian*, that if the public really knew the realities of the war, the war would have to finish the next day[15]. The Press Bureau censored all material voluntarily submitted by the press and circulated all official information. The Press Bureau was staffed by army censors; very few of whom had a background in journalism. Its function was to censor all information which might assist the enemy. This included all front line and naval news.

Many members of the press complained that the Bureau was incompetent and far too harsh. Lord Northcliffe (of the *Daily Mail*) complained that `... our people have nothing but the casualty lists and the mutilated scraps with which it is quite impossible to arouse interest or follow the war intelligently'[16]. The *New Statesman* argued that the Press Bureau should concern itself with preventing the publication of vital military information, but that broad and frank discussion on the conduct of the war was essential to maintain public support and morale. The *New Statesman* deliberately avoided criticising the rank and the file of the military, but was sometimes

---

[15] Lloyd George cited in Pilger, `The Myth-Makers', p33.
[16] Lord Northcliffe cited in A. Smith, `Censorship and the Great War', p193 in P. Hyland and H. Sammells (eds), *Writing and Censorship in Britain*, Routledge: London, 1992, pp185-199.

highly critical of military command. It avoided overt pacifism, gave general support to the war effort and opposed all attempts by the state to silence critical opinion[17].

The British government adopted similar methods during the Second World War. The Ministry of Information vetted all newsreels, BBC news programmes and the press. This was made relatively easy because news gathering was centralised. Both the Press Association and Reuters were located in the same building in Fleet Street. The Ministry of Information was therefore able to censor news before it reached the press. Censorship was often based upon `informal understandings', which allowed the government to create the illusion that the British media had more freedom and were far more reliable and accurate than the German media[18].

When Churchill became Prime Minister in May 1940, he set about using the radio (TV transmissions ceased for the duration of the war) to inspire the nation. He did not, however, trust the BBC. During the late 1930s, the BBC had followed Neville Chamberlain's policy of appeasement. Churchill was denied a platform because of his anti-German speeches, and because overt criticisms of fascism were excluded from BBC programmes. In 1938, Germany invaded Czechoslovakia; yet the BBC remained virtually silent on the event and instructed the Conservative MP Harold Nicholson that he could not refer to the invasion in his weekly broadcast. It transpired that his script had been vetoed by the Foreign Secretary. It has been argued that there existed a definite `conspiracy of silence'[19]. Churchill believed that the BBC was `one of the major neutrals' and considered assuming direct control by making it a branch of the Ministry of Information. It was decided, however, to rely upon indirect methods. Patrick Ryan, the BBC's Director of Home News, attended daily

---

[17] Smith, `Censorship and the Great War', p189, and pp 193-196.
[18] K. Williams, *Get me a murder a day !*, Arnold: London, 1998, pp138-140.
[19] *Auntie: The Inside Story of the BBC, Part 1 - 1922-1945*, BBC 1 (28.10.1997).

briefings by the Ministry of Information and all news concerning 'security and policy' was subject to official censorship[20].

The BBC continued to claim that it was accurate and objective, and it considered itself the 'voice of Britain'. The BBC attained increased significance because it could deliver up to date news far more effectively than the press. It was particularly important in spreading news about military campaigns. The BBC tended to follow the priorities of the government. Although it did not actively mislead the British people, many important stories were given low priority in line with government policy. News of the persecution of the Jews, for example, was never given priority because the BBC accepted the view of the government that the only effective solution relied upon the victory of the allies[21].

The government was intolerant of criticisms from the press. In the summer of 1940, the Home Secretary was given the power to ban any publication deemed to be of threat to the successful conclusion of the war[22]. The government banned both the *Daily Worker* and the *Week*. Both papers had a left wing slant. Although they had relatively small readerships, they were considered dangerous because of their criticisms of the government. This ban on the *Daily Worker* was not lifted until August 1942.[23]. The government even considered banning the *Daily Mirror* and *Sunday Pictorial* because of their criticisms of the government. The Home Secretary, Herbert Morrison, opposed any direct action against the papers because he believed that it is '... a tradition of the British people that they still remain obedient to the constituted authorities while retaining their liberty to ridicule and denounce the individuals who are actually in authority'[24]. As an alternative, the government used the Newspaper Proprietors Association to warn the owners of the papers concerned that unless their staff exercised some restraint, compulsory censorship would be

[20] *Auntie: The Inside Story of the BBC, Part I- 1922-1945*
[21] Seaton, 'Broadcasting History', pp141-143.
[22] Regulation 2D cited in Curran, 'Press History', p60.
[23] Curran, 'Press History', pp61-66.
[24] Herbert Morrison cited in Curran, 'Press History', p62.

imposed on both the *Daily Mirror* and the *Sunday Pictorial*. This was enough to moderate the content of the papers for a while. In 1942, however, the *Daily Mirror* launched a sustained attack on the government and claimed that it was foolish to tolerate the blunders of the existing administration. Morrison told the *Daily Mirror* that if it failed to recognise its `public responsibilities', it would be closed without further notice. This effectively silenced the radicalism of the *Daily Mirror* for the duration of the war[25].

Throughout the war, the press and broadcasters were responsible for maintaining the morale of the nation and for revitalising the `national spirit' following the Dunkirk retreat of June 1940. The public was not told the truth about the retreat. Instead, it was presented as a triumph. The BBC transmitted a moving account of the retreat by J.B. Priestly which, with considerable eloquence, `snatched glory out of defeat'[26]. Tom Hopkinson, editor of the *Picture Post*, recalled that it was important to conceal the truth of `external reality' with the `truth of the imagination'. In his view, this `spiritual truth' of events should be emphasised for `... in wartime there is something more important than truth'[27]. Reports dealing with the progress of the war were consistently positive. Frank Gillard, a radio reporter for the BBC, recalls how when British troops were involved in an unsuccessful invasion of Dieppe, his censored report neglected to deal with the failure and the casualties, and concentrated instead upon his praise for the excellent air support. It was not until the Spring of 1945, that realism was allowed in war reports and allied as well as enemy casualties were acknowledged[28].

The selective presentation of information was also important in creating domestic support for the war and in producing the `myth' or illusion of war time unity. The function of the Ministry of Information was to present a picture of unity and to conceal such

---

[25] Curran, `Press History', pp63-66.

[26] *Auntie: The Inside Story of the BBC, Part 1- 1922-1945*

[27] Tom Hopkinson cited in Williams, `Something more important than truth', p154.

[28] *Auntie: The Inside Story of the BBC, Part 1 - 1922-1945.*

things as class divisions. In this, it had the support of the mainstream media. All news which threatened this image was suppressed. The presence of industrial conflict, for example, was not reported in the media. Industrial discontent increased during the war. In 1944 alone, 6 million working days were lost as a result of industrial disputes. Without first hand knowledge of these disputes, many people assumed the existence of industrial peace. Problems surrounding the inadequate provision of air raid shelters were also concealed. News of a serious accident in which 173 people died during a stampede to get into the shelter at Bethnal Green Tube Station was suppressed in the interests of morale, and remained an Official Secret until the 1970s. The Mass Observation Survey conducted research on public perceptions of safety in public air raid shelters. It found that the vast majority of the population felt that the shelters were unsafe. Rather than improve the provision of shelters, the Ministry of Information published leaflets claiming that the shelters were safe[29].

There tends to be a high level of direct and official censorship during total wars. This is justified on the grounds that the survival of the nation is at stake. If Britain had lost either of the two world wars, it would have been occupied by its former enemy and subject to financial and legal recriminations. This is often deemed enough to justify tight control over the media and other dissident voices. The government, however, have no right to expect total support for its actions. Official censorship can easily backfire, especially when it contradicts the experiences of the general public. Once there is doubt concerning the credibility of official sources of information, then rumour becomes more important and public confidence is shaken. Total wars may well require a unified national effort, but this is rarely created through censorship and deceit.

Censorship and limited wars

Limited wars are those involving only a small section of the population. These wars often involve invading other countries for

---

[29] Nick Tiratsoo in *Myths and Memories of World War 2*, BBC 2 (July 1995).

economic or political gains, rather than because our own immediate safety is at stake. The so-called 'policing' actions of the cold war fall into this category, as does western military action against the gulf states and in parts of central Europe. Britain has been involved in a number of these limited wars. It participated in the Korean War of the 1950s, fought nationalist movements in its own disintegrating empire, and has recently been involved in the war in Kosovo. Two examples of limited wars will be covered in what follows: the Falklands War of 1982 and the Gulf War of 1991.

Apart from military information, there was no official censorship during the Falklands War. Relations between the media and the government, however, deteriorated significantly. It was evident that the government expected a far higher level of voluntary and self censorship, and did all it could to frustrate the media's task of gathering reliable information. Brian McNair has argued that media coverage during the Falklands War was '... among the most restricted of all post Second World War conflicts'[30]. Robert Harris has argued likewise that that there was extensive government and military tampering with the information journalists could broadcast, and that the Ministry of Defence '... could regulate the flow of pictures and deodorise the war in a way that few democratic governments - especially recent administrations in the USA - have been able to get away with'[31].

Britain's involvement in the Falklands, like America's involvement in Vietnam, did not receive unanimous support from Parliament and the general public. While the task force was still en route to the Falklands, the BBC transmitted a Panorama programme entitled *Can we avoid war ?* This programme discussed the possibility of a diplomatic solution and included contributions from dissident Conservative MPs. George Howell and Alisdair Milne of the BBC were summoned to Downing Street to explain themselves to Mrs Thatcher, and were accused of heading a left wing conspiracy to bring

---

[30] McNair, *An Introduction to Political Communication*, p174.
[31] Robert Harris cited in McNair, *An Introduction to Political Communication*, p174.

down the government. It was also accused of dishonouring the British tradition of freedom of speech, and of incompetent supervision and control over its programme makers[32].

Coverage of the fighting was censored during the Falklands War by army and navy officers. All reports were viewed and scrutinised on the basis of 'taste'. Broadcasters, in particular, were urged to minimise the human cost of the war by excluding pictures of death and avoiding the use of graphic language to describe the horrors of death. The media had difficulties, at the outset, gaining access to the navy whose co-operation was essential. The naval command declared that it would allow no journalists to travel with the Falklands task force. Bernard Ingham, Mrs. Thatcher's press secretary, recognised that this could harm the war effort, and that negative publicity should be avoided at all costs. As a result of his intervention, 28 journalists were allowed to go with the task force[33]. The media found, however, that the navy remained obstructive. The media had no problem accepting censorship on security matters, but journalists were also prevented from reporting on anything which might have harmful effects upon the morale of the troops, or show these troops in a negative light. They were prevented, for example, from showing the troops swearing or fighting among themselves[34].

Broadcasters in Britain complained that they were too restricted. ITN argued that it could have given more support for the war, had the restrictions been relaxed. In addition to censoring individual reports, the military delayed the release of visual footage of the war. The Ministry of Defence believed that pictures of the war would disturb people, as they had done during the Vietnam War. There was, at times, a delay of 23 days between the event and the eventual transmission. The military achieved this level of obstruction by controlling all material sent by satellite. The broadcast media had to resort to using quick sketch artists to illustrate their stories. Under

---

[32] Williams, 'Something more important than the truth', p162 and *Auntie; The Inside Story of the BBC, Part 4- 1970-1986.*

[33] McNair, *An Introduction to Political Communication*, p175.

[34] McNair, *An Introduction to Political Communication*, p176.

these conditions, the use of and popularity of radio became particularly important in reporting the war[35].

Broadcasters in Britain also reported on the families of the task force. It was felt that the Falklands War was too remote to sustain interest. Telling the story of families separated by the war thus helped to bridge the gap. According to the Glasgow University Media Group, these families were `... presented as models of support for the war but were largely denied the possibility of expressing their own opinions and doubts'[36]. This coverage concentrated upon the emotions of the families towards the soldier, rather than the thoughts of the families on the nature and legitimacy of the war. The BBC decided not to interview the families of those killed in the war, and argued that its decision stemmed from its concern for privacy and taste. The Glasgow Group, however, claim that `... the effect was to silence those who could have told us most directly about the human costs of the fighting, and to censor any doubts they may have had about whether the fighting was worthwhile'[37]. Although some of the media were critical of the war, many saw the war in terms of a human interest story and thereby helped to create a myth of the war for the general public. This `human interest story' had a sexual angle. The media included coverage of a scantily clad woman delivering a singing telegram to the troops, close ups of women dancing for the troops, the troops `chatting up' women nurses, features on a stewardess on the QE2 which transported the troops to the Falklands, and stories about the clothes that women soldiers would wear whilst on the Falklands. Women involved in the conflict were presented as a `sexual interest'[38].

[35] Williams, `Something more important than the truth', pp 159-162 and *Auntie: The Inside Story of the BBC, Part 4- 1970-1986.*
[36] Glasgow University Media Group, `The Falklands Conflict: The Home Front', p430 in P. Marris and S. Thornham (eds), *Media Studies: A Reader*, Edinburgh University Press: Edinburgh, 1996, pp 430-437.
[37] Glasgow Media Group, `The Falklands Conflict: The Home Front', p433.
[38] Glasgow University Media Group, `The Falklands Conflict: The Home Front', p437.

The Falklands War, like the Vietnam War, was sold to the domestic population as a fight against tyranny. Unlike the Second World War, it did not involve the majority of the domestic population; the fighting was remote and the clarity of purpose rather less compelling. The British government vied for support and showed itself to be intolerant of criticism. It controlled the media to a greater extent than America had done during the Vietnam War and, to some extent, justified this on the basis of learning from America's mistakes. This policy did, however, backfire upon the government. As journalists were deprived of information and denied off the record briefings, they were left without any real guidance. They reported on what they saw and heard, and even speculated. This resulted in some serious leaks of military information[39].

During the Gulf War of 1991, the military exerted direct control over information. Censorship and propaganda was used by both sides. Saddam Hussein emphasised the horrors of civilian casualties, whilst the allies concentrated upon the effectiveness of the military campaign. In an article written for *The Guardian* in March 1991, Philip Knightley argued that allied propaganda aimed to sanitise the war. He claimed that propaganda during wartime has generally aimed to deprive the enemy of useful information and to secure public support. During the Gulf War, however, a new element was added: to change the way we view war and convince us that new technology took away the horrors of warfare. Military briefings talked of 'surgical' strikes which demolished military targets whilst limiting civilian casualties. The impression gained from these briefings was that it was a war carried out by intelligent machines rather than fought by people. The military gained support for this interpretation by using a pool system which excluded maverick reporters from the briefings in favour of those who were considered more 'reliable'[40]. Many members of the media were willing to accept the restrictions of the

---

[39] McNair, *An Introduction to Political Communication*, p177.
[40] P. Knightley, 'Sanitising the News', pp315-316 in B. Macarthur (ed), *Despatches from the Gulf War*, pp314-317, and B. Macarthur, 'Introduction', pxviii in Macarthur (ed), *Despatches from the Gulf War*, ppxv-xxi.

pool system, knowing that the alternative was to be excluded and risk losing access to information. Robert Fisk, of the *Independent*, stayed out of the pool system. He negotiated his own way to the front lines, and tended to be critical of reporters who settled for the ease of the military briefings. Fisk argued that `... so dependent have journalists become upon information dispensed by the Western military authorities in Saudi Arabia, so enamoured of their technology, that press and television reporters have found themselves trapped'[41].

Certain information was restricted; including details about the number of troops involved, outlines of future plans, locations of military forces, methods of warfare, origin of aircraft support, and any information that could be used against allied forces. Journalists received most of their information from carefully staged briefings held by General Norman Schwarzkopf, and all of their material was screened by military censors. They were kept away from the troops as much as possible. In Dhahran, the Joint Information Bureau provided the media with video footage of aerial strikes against Iraq. Journalists maintained the right to appeal against the decisions of the military censors, but the time spent on such reviews would tend to make the news item out of date and thus deprive it of news value[42].

The Ministry of Defence reinforced official censorship by keeping track of all news stories on the Gulf, and writing to any editor who published material which met with the disapproval of the military[43]. The BBC was criticised by the government and by tabloids on the right. Following its coverage of Iraq's civilian casualties, it was condemned by the *Sun*, the *Daily Express* and the *Daily Mail* for biased reporting. This gained support from such Conservative MPs as

---

[41] Robert Fisk cited in Snoddy, *The Good, the Bad and the Unacceptable*, pp58-59. See also McNair, *An Introduction to Political Communication*, pp182-183.

[42] K. Williams, `The Light at The End of the Tunnel: The Mass Media, Public Opinion and the Vietnam War', p306 in J. Eldridge (ed), *Getting the Message*, Routledge: London, 1993, pp305-328, C. Lamay, M. Fitzsimon, and J. Sahadi (eds), *The Media at War,* Columbia University Press: New York, 1991, p3 and pp18-19, McNair, *An Introduction to Political Communication*, p182.

[43] Knightley, `Sanitising the News', p317.

Nicholas Soames, Jonathan Sayeed and Dudley Smith[44]. There was a high level of support for the war in the House of Commons and amongst the general public. Opinion polls showed that 80% of British people were in favour of the war against Iraq[45]. There was, however, some popular resistance to the management of news during the war. According to research carried out by Martin Shaw and Roy Carr-Hill, many people in Britain felt that the media had glorified the war[46].

The Gulf War shows that, in spite of developments in technology, the media have become more scrutinised and controlled by the state during times of war. John Simpson claimed that it was 'depressing' that demands were being made for journalists to participate in the propaganda process rather than promote an open and honest understanding of the war[47]. There are no real signs that the British state is becoming more liberal in its attitude towards wartime reporting. It appears willing to suppress the right of the individual to state facts (and in some cases critical opinion), and justifies this oppression on the grounds of national security. This rationale states that when a nation goes to war, the rights of the individual are necessarily subordinated to the welfare of the nation.

The state exerts less direct control over the media during limited wars than during total wars, but still has ways to control the information we receive. The state does not have to resort to censorship; it can obstruct and bully the media to support the war effort and avoid any real critical coverage. The media are used to sanitise the war by showing the nation's troops in the best light, by avoiding coverage of death and by creating the impression that wars are fought with intelligence and precision. The media rely increasingly upon military briefings which minimise the suffering in war zones, and upon covering the impact of war upon the families left behind by the troops. The tabloids are prone to abandon any real

---

[44] Harris, 'Don't Shoot the Messenger', pp142-143.
[45] Macarthur, 'Introduction', pxvii.
[46] See Michael Morgan, 'Introduction: The Media and the Persian Gulf War', *Electronic Journal of Communication*, Volume 2, no 1, December 1991, pp4-5.
[47] J. Simpson cited in Williams, 'Something more important than truth', p168.

scrutiny of wars, and can be relied upon for their open patriotic support. In this they seem to reflect and reinforce the attitudes of the general public.

Conclusion

The state finds it easier to restrict the media during times of war. It can appeal to the common interest, warn about the dangers of 'enemies within', show generally high levels of public support for wars, manipulate the fears of the general public, and accuse dissident voices of supporting the 'enemy' and of holding the lives of the nation's troops in contempt. The state recognises that the media have a particularly important role in creating public attitudes towards a war. McNair argues that '... governments have to 'manufacture' consent for the pursuit of war, and manage opinion in such a way that the war aims are achieved'[48]. This has led some people to believe that journalists should be patriotic during times of war. Max Hastings claims that journalists have a duty to take into account the 'national interest', whilst John Pilger complains that the idea of the 'national interest' is far too vague that too few journalists question the motives which lie behind the wars we wage[49]. The state expects the media to abandon their scrutinising role and to do all they can to bolster morale and convince the public that we are fighting a just war. Journalists risk ostracism and state coercion for speaking out or even questioning the actions of a wartime government. When a state obstructs or prohibits debate on the motives behind a war and prohibits scrutiny of command decisions, it deceives the public and does a disservice to those who risk their lives for the nation.

---

[48] McNair, *An Introduction to Political Communication*, p169.
[49] J. Pilger, 'The Myth-Makers' p34.

9. Conclusion

This book has been concerned with the freedom and responsibilities of the British media. It has been argued that a free media is not necessarily good in itself, and that the media should assume some social responsibilities. The media produce something that is consumed by the vast majority of people in this country. The media influence the views we have, and help to shape our society. The British media attract their fair share of critics. Michael Nicholson of ITN, who is about to retire from broadcasting, has recently complained that the BBC in particular is guilty of boring and trivialised news and that `... every aspect of the media is moving towards trivialising, showbizzing, and infotainment'[1]. Harold Evans, the former editor of the *Sunday Times*, claims that the public trust in the media has been harmed by excessive media intrusion, malice, and invention and that a `... delinquent press diminishes, and diminishes logarithmically, freedom and democracy'[2]. But what, if anything, can be done to encourage the media to assume their social responsibilities.

Advocates of the free market warn against tampering with the freedom of the press. David Gordon argues that abuses in freedom of expression and of the press are unfortunate, but should not be used to undermine the right of free expression. There should not be limits placed upon freedom of expression, even in the name of ethics. He argued against allowing the regulation of the media and the curtailment of freedom of expression. In his view, ethics rather than legal control should nurture responsibility in the media. People in the media need the freedom to choose where their responsibilities lie; this is the essence of any meaningful ethics. He claimed that `... mass media ethics must be based on a "first principle" that ensures zealous protection for freedom of expression while leaving us fallible mortals

---

[1] Michael Nicholson cited in Duncan, `If more reporters showed emotion, TV news wouldn't be losing so many viewers', p12.
[2] Harold Evans cited in Snoddy, *The Good, the Bad and the Unacceptable*, p201.

free to chart our own ethical (or unethical) courses, guided by our own principles regarding responsibility'[3]. He argues that responsible or ethical behaviour cannot and should not be enforced because the *duty* of responsibility cannot be derived from the *right* to free expression. Freedom of expression must be protected. Gordon claims that we can use this right to argue against irresponsible behaviour, but we would threaten freedom of expression if we attempt to enforce responsible or ethical behaviour[4].

Those who are vehement in their defense of freedom of the media tend to argue that the free market should be protected and advanced because it gives consumers what they want. Rupert Murdoch, for example, claims that `... anybody who, within the law of the land, provides a service which the public wants at a price it can afford is providing a public service'[5]. Such sentiments were echoed by the New Right and the Thatcher government of the 1980s. The New Right argue that public regulation of the media amounts to a form of censorship, and that the consumer needs greater freedom of choice. Individuals are thought to be the best judge of what they read or see, and it is argued that no person or committee has the right to impose its own values and claim superiority in the choices it makes[6]. The Peacock Committee of 1985 argued in favour of extending consumer choice in broadcasting, and against any pre-publication (or Broadcasting) censorship. It argued against regulating broadcasting, but claimed that a new body (the Public Service Broadcasting Council) should lend support or patronage to worthy projects, and be funded out of the license fee and from the fees paid by ITV contractors[7].

It is clear that whether we like it or not, the media are subject to market pressures and that this will affect the content and tone of the media. Raymond Snoddy claims that there are no universal or

---

[3] A.D. Gordon in Gordon and Kittross, *Controversies in Media Ethics*, p27.
[4] Gordon in Gordon and Kittross, *Controversies in Media Ethics*, p32.
[5] Keane, *The Media and Democracy*, p121.
[6] Samuel Brittan cited in Negrine, *Politics and the Mass Media in Britain*, p34.
[7] Negrine, *Politics and the Mass Media in Britain*, p35.

unchanging standards in journalism, and what we regard as acceptable will change over time. In his view, the `... content of newspapers reflects society's values at any particular time, and, while newspapers may speed up and spread social change, they rarely succeed against the trend'[8]. Some papers with worthy aims have failed to capture a market. The *News on Sunday*, for example, was established in 1986 as a left-of-centre tabloid, with a commitment to combating sexism, racism and fascism. Within a year, it faced a severe financial crisis and was unable to continue. The *Sunday Sport*, on the other hand, did not go for the moral high ground, and catered to a demand for soft-core pornography. This shows, amongst other things, that the market influences or even determines what the media can do[9]. This market pressure is made all the worse by the growth of international media networks. Negrine argues that the amount of capital required to set up and to survive international competition makes it difficult for small or independent media groups. The growth of the international media will, over time, affect the operations of the media in each country. The ideas of balance and impartiality, for example, have special meaning for the British media but `... in the international context these notions and their attendant practices will appear meaningless'[10].

The market in which the media operate is increasingly fragmented and specialised. The broadcast media in particular is being changed by the spread of cable and satellite stations. In order to compete, terrestrial television is adopting a more tabloid style and losing some of its serious edge. Stuart Purvis of ITN has argued that an increase in `popular' items on news programmes will not harm democracy as it makes these programmes more attractive to the public[11]. Richard Sambrook of BBC News has argued likewise that increased choice in news programmes have forced broadcasters to become more tabloid in style to attract audiences[12]. The alternative, however, is to force cable

---

[8] Snoddy, *The Good, the Bad and the Unacceptable*, p18.
[9] Negrine, *Politics and the Mass Media in Britain*, p24,
[10] Negrine, *Politics and the Mass Media in Britain*, p29. See also p28.
[11] Stewart Purvis interviewed in *News and the Democratic Agenda.*
[12] Richard Sambrook interviewed in *News and the Democratic Agenda.*

and satellite to take on some responsibility for public service broadcasting. The independent documentary maker Roger Bolton, for example, argues that *Sky* is making extraordinary profits, and that the government should expect *Sky* to include some quality documentaries and current affairs programmes. He argues that without such regulation, independent journalism and the scrutiny of government action is under threat[13].

A de-regulated, free market media does not necessarily mean that the media are less censored or restricted. Although the state might have less effective control over the media, the owners of the media have developed their own censorial powers. They determine the range of views that will be aired and in doing so they restrict access to the free exchange of ideas and opinions. The media are concerned with what is commercially viable. They do not respond to the needs of the citizen, but to the market and tastes they create for themselves. According to John Keane, people are `... treated as market-led consumers, not as active citizens with rights and obligations'[14]. Ralph Negrine has argued that the dominance of market forces turn the content of the media into commodities rather than something produced to enrich the public good. This, he argues, leads to less diversity and a poorer product because the media have to chase the same audiences. This is bad for minorities and for society as a whole. He argues that the media are far too important to be left to the fluctuations of the market[15].

The media are increasingly under the control of a small number of corporations which have reduced the diversity of their product and undermined public control. The high costs of setting up news media ventures ensure that it remains under the control of an elite. It is estimated that it costs in the region of £20 million to establish a daily newspaper, and that to set up a new cable station costs approximately £30 million. According to James Curran, this has created `... a zone of influence in which dominant economic forces have a privileged

---

[13] Roger Bolton interviewed in *News and the Democratic Agenda*.
[14] Keane, *The Media and Democracy*, p91. See also pp90-91.
[15] Negrine, *Politics and the Mass Media in Britain*, pp36-37.

position, and to which other significant social forces are denied direct, unmediated access'[16]. Although there has been a dramatic increase in the number of television channels, this has not done anything significant to increase the ideological diversity of views expressed. The consumers have more choice, but the ideological diet remains largely unaltered[17]. Curran argues that the free marketeers overstate the extent to which the media corporations are themselves slaves of the market. In his view, they do not constantly subordinate their own ideological preferences, and the consumer does not have ultimate power in determining the content of the media. The modern media has a large bureaucratic structure which interprets, reflects and resists audience pressure[18].

Democracy is not served well by an un-regulated media. The market can and does hamper the free flow of diverse opinions and information. Market pressures encourage news organisations to present the news in line with the supposed dominant values of their audiences. It could well be that the truth is sacrificed in the interests of reinforcing (or at least not challenging) the core of these values. The free market does little to cultivate an informed and critical citizen body because news organisations rarely stray from the dominant beliefs of their target group. Although diverse views are sometimes expressed in the media, many media organisations show little interest in encouraging democratic debate[19].

If broadcasters are to serve democracy, they must have some commitment to public service programming. Jonathan Powell of the BBC described public service media as a commitment to mixed programming, guided by the need to go beyond mere entertainment. Public service broadcasting aims to produce quality programmes which reflect the diversity of human experience and enhance our quality of life[20]. Those who believe that the media should be guided

---

[16] Curran, 'Mass Media and Democracy Revisited', p94.
[17] Curran, 'Mass Media and Democracy Revisited', p94.
[18] Curran, 'Mass Media and Democracy Revisited', pp94-96.
[19] O'Neill, 'Journalism in the market place', p15, p18, pp21-23 and p26.
[20] Keane, The Media and Democracy, p117.

by the demands of the market regard public service commitments as a threat to their freedom. It has been argued, however, that we are too accustomed to regard freedom as freedom *from the state* rather than seeing it as freedom *for* such things as diversity and equal access to the media. Although it is important to avoid state control, we must also recognise that the media should have a role in serving the `public interest'[21].

Public service broadcasting should attempt to scrutinise and place limits upon those with power. It should be open to diverse sections of society and encourage `... an open, tolerant and lively society in which great big dogmas and smelly little orthodoxies of all kinds are held in check'[22]. A truly public service media can help make policy makers more accountable, and place limits upon the exercise of political power. It can serve as an `early warning device' and as a way of checking the `unending arrogance and foolishness' of those who have effective power[23]. The media can also serve the public interest by exposing the public to a diverse range of views. Curran believes that the media should broaden the values and perspectives expressed in both entertainment and current affairs programmes. It is only through acquainting people with diverse perspectives that they can have a variety of sources from which to deliberate on public affairs. It is important that diverse social groups have access to information and access to the media so that they can express their views. These groups should be encouraged to take a more active part in public life. The media needs to present people with a diverse range of choices and continue to exert pressure on the powers that be by giving diverse social groups a clear and effective channel of influence[24].

The public interest is not served simply by a free media, but by a responsible media. Carol Reuss argues that the media must be made to exercise its freedom in an ethical way. The media should be concerned with the content and effects of its product. Freedom and

---

[21] Negrine, *Politics and the Mass Media in Britain*, p27.
[22] Keane, *The Media and Democracy*, p167.
[23] Keane, *The Media and Democracy*, pp176-181.
[24] Curran, `Mass Media and Democracy Revisited', pp103-104.

responsibility, she claimed, should not be seen as opposites. Real freedom flows from a sense of personal responsibility[25]. In Britain, there have been numerous attempts to encourage journalists to behave in a responsible manner and to get the media to assume their social responsibilities. The 1949 Commission on the Press called for the formation of the Press Council in the hope of encouraging in the press a greater sense of public responsibility and public service. According to Curran, however, the relaxation of newsprint controls at the end of the war fuelled competition between the papers and led to a press which was 'more sensationalist and irresponsible'[26]. The 1977 Commission on the Press stated that the press needed to act with more restraint, be guided by the ideals of public service, and provide proper training for journalists which took into account questions about the nature of society not only journalism skills. The commission was, however, caught in a series of contradictions. In particular, it wanted the press to behave as a public service and for journalists to adopt a more balanced and responsible approach, whilst avoiding overt public regulation of the press. Curran believes that these principles are contradictory, and that this explains the lack of success the Commission had in promoting its ideals[27].

Increasing the social responsibility of the media may well be hampered by increased centralisation of ownership of the press. Negrine argues that this tendency shows that it is unlikely that social responsibility can be increased unless the media are forced to assume new obligations and duties to society[28]. Curran and Seaton have argued that the media must be made more representative and responsible. They claim that the media should be forced to express a broader diversity of cultural and ideological views. The tendency towards monopoly ownership of the media must be countered, and new media ventures should be given financial assistance. This

---

[25] Carol Reuss in Gordon and Kittross, *Controversies in Media Ethics*, pp32-34.
[26] J. Curran, 'The Liberal Theory of Press Freedom' p296 in J. Curran and J. Seaton, *Power Without Responsibility*, Routledge: London, 1997, pp287-301.
[27] Curran, 'The Liberal Theory of Press Freedom', p298.
[28] Negrine, *Politics and the Media in Britain*, p32.

funding could be raised by placing a levy on advertising[29]. The media must be made more responsible to society. The social responsibilities of the media could include such things as providing information to the public, creating a forum for democratic discussion, representing and expressing a diversity of opinions, and protecting our civil rights against encroachments by the state[30].

Both the free market and social responsibility theories of the media recognise that it is important for the media to maintain the freedom to publish free from excessive censorship, but differ significantly in the way they view regulation of the media and indeed the product of the media. The free market approach wants to regulate against over centralisation of power, whilst the social responsibility approach wants to regulate in favour of diversity and plurality. The product of the media is also viewed in different ways. The free market approach tends to view the product of the media as a `commodity', whereas the social responsibility approach views it as something contributing to the public good[31].

Those interested in the future of the media are faced with two main ideologies. The free market approach states that freedom of expression and a free media are necessary to serve democracy. All attempts to control the media hamper the media's scrutinising functions. The free market approach denies that the media have ultimate responsibility for their product. It claims that the media are merely responding to public demand and have no control (or interest) in the social consequences of their product. The globalised media market, moreover, make it difficult (if not impossible) for national governments to regulate the media or impose social responsibilities. The free market approach argues that the consumer is sovereign. Consumers should be free to purchase whatever media they wish. The broader their choice of newspapers, magazines and television channels the better. If the consumer wishes to buy sensationalist

---

[29] Negrine, *Politics and the Mass Media in Britain*, p33.
[30] Lacey and Longman, *The Press as Public Educator*, pp23-24.
[31] Negrine, *Politics and the Mass Media in Britain*, p37.

media, they should be free to do so. Any attempt to regulate the media is seen as a threat to the freedom of the individual.

The public service approach argues that the private ownership and control of the media limits the range of views we receive and encourages widespread apathy. Advocates of a public service media tend to argue that the media have definite social responsibilities. These include such things as monitoring the actions of a government, fuelling democratic debate by exposing the public to a diverse range of views, and serving the *public interest* rather than responding to the *interests of the public*. This approach recognises that journalists should not simply respond to the market, but that they have a range of responsibilities. It is not acceptable for journalists to deny responsibility for what they produce and to blame the public for buying scurrilous material. They help to create the market, they are not its slaves.

Unless the media assume their social responsibilities, they run the risk of having these responsibilities imposed upon them. Some journalists avoid responsibility by deferring to the dictates of the market. This is not a sufficient justification. Social responsibility is enhanced not by increasing the number of regulations and laws that control the media, but by the media recognising and furthering their role in the democratic process and by taking responsibility for what is produced. Journalists are not mere conduits through which information is transmitted to the public. They help to create the image we have of other citizens. They have the power to combat prejudice, expose injustices and make the government accountable to the people. Responsible journalists recognise that they are part of the community, and use their position to further the public interest.

166

Bibliography

Archard, D., `Privacy, the public interest and a prurient public', in M. Kieran (ed), *Media Ethics*, Routledge: London, 1998, pp82-96.

Baehr, H., and Spindler-Brown, A., `Firing a Broadside: A Feminist intervention into mainstream TV', in H. Baehr and A. Gray (eds), *Turning it on*, Arnold: London, 1996, pp183-189.

Barendt, E., *Freedom of Speech*, Clarendon: Oxford, 1985.

Barker, M., *The New Racism*, Junction Books: London, 1981.

Bell, M., `The Journalism of Attachment', in M. Kieran (ed), *Media Ethics*, Routledge: London, 1998, pp15-22.

Belsey, A., `Privacy, Publicity and Politics', in A. Belsey and R. Chadwick (eds), *Ethical Issues in Journalism and the Media*, Routledge: London, 1992, pp77-92.

Belsey, A., and Chadwick, R., `Ethics and Politics of the Media', in A. Belsey and R. Chadwick (eds), *Ethical Issues in Journalism and the Media*, Routledge: London, 1992, pp1-14.

Belsey, A., `Journalism and Ethics: Can they co-exist ?', in M. Kieran (ed), *Media Ethics*, Routledge: London, 1998, pp1-14.

Blue, A., `Censorship - An analysis', in G. Chester and J. Dickey (eds), *Feminism and Censorship: The Current Debate*, Prism Press: Dorset, 1988, pp52-61.

Cohen, E.D. (ed), *Philosophical Issues in Journalism*, OUP: New York, 1992.

Cottle, S., `Ethnic Minorities in the British News Media', in J. Stokes and A. Reading (eds), *The Media in Britain*, Macmillan: Houndmills, 1999.

Curran, J., `Mass Media and Democracy Revisited', in J. Curran and M. Gurevitch (eds), *Mass Media and Society*, Arnold: London, 1996, pp81-115.

Curran, J., `Press History', in J. Curran and J. Seaton, *Power Without Responsibility*, Routledge: London, 1997, pp5-108.

Curran, J., The Liberal Theory of Press Freedom', in J. Curran and J. Seaton, *Power Without Responsibility*, Routledge: London, 1997, pp287-301.

Daniel, S., `Some conflicting assumptions about journalistic ethics', in E.D. Cohen (ed), *Philosophical Issues in Journalism*, OUP: New York, 1992, pp50-59.

Dickey, J., and Chester, G., `Introduction', in G. Chester and J. Dickey (eds), *Feminism and Censorship: The Current Debate*, Prism Press: Dorset, 1988, pp1-10.

Dorey, P., *British Politics since 1945*, Blackwell: Oxford, 1995.

Downing, J., *The Media Machine*, Pluto: London, 1980.

Dummett, M. and Dummett, A., `The Role of Government in Britain's Racial Crisis', p113 in C. Husband (ed), *Race in Britain: Continuity and Change*, Hutchinson Education: London, 1987, pp111-141.

Edgar, A., `Objectivity, bias and the truth', in A. Belsey and R. Chadwick (eds), *Ethical Issues in Journalism and the Media*, Routledge: London, 1992, pp112-129.

Edgerton, G., `Quelling the Oxygen of Publicity', *Journal of Popular Culture*, Volume 30, no 1, Summer 1996, pp115-131.

Eldridge, J., Kitzinger, J., and Williams, K., *The Mass Media Power in Modern Britain*, Oxford University Press: Oxford, 1997.

Enzenberger, H.M., `The industrialisation of the Mind', in H. Enzenberger, *Raids and Reconstructions*, Pluto: London, 1976.

Feldman, D., *Civil Liberties and Human Rights in England and Wales*, Oxford University Press: Oxford, 1993, p388.

Franklin, B., and Pilling, R., `Market, moguls and media regulation', in M. Kieran (ed), *Media Ethics*, Routledge: London, 1998, pp111-122.

Gilbert, P., `The Oxygen of Publicity', in A. Belsey and R. Chadwick (eds), *Ethical Issues in Journalism and the Media*, Routledge: London, 1992, pp137-153.

Gill, R., `Ideology, gender and popular radio' in H. Baehr and A. Gray (eds), *Turning it on*, Arnold: London, 1996, pp211-217.

Gilroy, P., *There aint no black in the Union Jack*, Hutchinson: London, 1987.

Glasser, T., 'Objectivity and news bias', in E.D. Cohen (ed), *Philosophical Issues in Journalism*, Oxford University Press: New York, 1992, pp176-185.

Golding, P., and Elliott, P., 'Bias, objectivity and ideology', in P. Marris and S. Thornham (eds), *Media Studies: A Reader*, Edinburgh University Press: Edinburgh, 1996, pp411-415.

Gordon, A.D., and Kittross, J., *Controversies in Media Ethics*, Longman: London, 1999.

Hall, S., 'Racist Ideologies and the Media', in P. Marris and S. Thornham (eds), *Media Studies: A Reader*, Edinburgh University Press: Edinburgh, 1996, pp160-168.

Harris, N., 'Codes of Conduct for Journalists', in A. Belsey and R. Chadwick (eds), *Ethical Issues in Journalism and the Media*, Routledge: London, 1992, pp62-76.

Glasgow University Media Group, 'The Falklands Conflict: The Home Front', in P. Marris and S. Thornham (eds), *Media Studies: A Reader*, Edinburgh University Press: Edinburgh, 1996, pp430-437.

Herman, E., and Chomsky, N., *Manufacturing Consent*, Vintage: London, 1994.

Heywood, A., *Political Ideologies*, Macmillan: London, 1992.

Holland, P., 'When a woman reads the news', in H. Baehr and A. Gray (eds), *Turning it on*, Arnold: London, 1996, pp195-199.

Itzin, C. (ed), *Pornography*, OUP: Oxford, 1992.

Keane, J., *The Media and Democracy*, Polity/Blackwell: Cambridge, 1991 (1994 edition).

Kelly, L., 'The US Ordinances: Censorship or radical law reform', in G. Chester and J. Dickey (eds), *Feminism and Censorship: The Current Debate*, Prism Press: Dorset, 1988, pp52-61.

Kieran, M., 'Objectivity, impartiality and good journalism', in M. Kieran (ed), *Media Ethics*, Routledge: London, 1998, pp23-36.

Lacey, C., and Longman, D., *The Press as Public Educator*, University of Luton Press: Luton, 1997.

Lamay, C., Fitzsimon, M., and Sahadi, J (eds), *The Media at War*, Columbia University Press: New York, 1991.

Lukes, S., *Individualism*, Blackwell: Oxford, 1973.

Macarthur, B., 'Introduction' to *Despatches from the Gulf War*, Bloomsbury: London, 1991, ppxv-xxi.

Madgwick, P.J., Steeds, D., and Williams, L., *Britain since 1945*, Hutchinson: London, 1982.

Marcuse, H., 'Repressive Tolerance', in R. Woolf, B. Moore and H. Marcuse, *A Critique of Pure Tolerance*, Cape: London, 1969.

McNair, B., *An Introduction to Political Communication*, Routledge: London, 1995.

McNair, B., *News and Journalism in the UK*, Routledge: London, 1994 (1996 edition).

McNair, B., 'Journalism, politics and public relations', in M. Kieran (ed), *Media Ethics*, Routledge: London, 1998, pp49-65.

Mendus, S., 'The Tigers of Wrath and the Horses of Instruction', in B. Parekh (ed), *Free Speech*, Commission for Racial Equality: London, 1990, pp3-17.

Merck, M., 'Sexism in the Media ?', in C. Gardner (ed), *Media, Politics and Culture*, Macmillan: London, 1979, pp95-107.

Mill, J.S., *On Liberty* in S. Collini (ed), *On Liberty and Other Writings*, Cambridge University Press: Cambridge, 1989, pp1-116.

Mill, J.S., 'Law of Libel and Liberty of the Press' (1825) in G.L. Williams (ed), *John Stuart Mill on Politics and Society*, Fontana: 1976, pp143-169.

Morgan, M., 'Introduction: The Media and the Persian Gulf War', *Electronic Journal of Communication*, Volume 2, no 1, December 1991, pp4-5.

Negrine, R., *Politics and the Mass Media in Britain*, Routledge: London, 1994.

Neilson, S., 'Books for bad women: A feminist look at censorship', in G. Chester and J. Dickey (eds), *Feminism and Censorship: The Current Debate*, Prism Books: Dorset, 1988, pp17-25.

Neustatter, A., *Hyenas in Petticoats*, Penguin: Harmondsworth, 1989 (1990 edition).

Okin, S.M., 'Gender, the Public and the Private', in D. Held (ed), *Political Theory Today*, Polity: Cambridge, 1991, pp67-90.

O'Leary, B., and McGarry, *The Politics of Antagonism*, The Athlone Press: London, 1993.

O'Neill, J., 'Journalism in the Market Place' in A. Belsey and R. Chadwick (eds), *Ethical Issues in Journalism and the Media*, Routledge: London, 1992, pp15-32.

Owen, J., 'Documentary and Citizenship: The Case of Stephen Lawrence', in J. Stokes and A. Reading (eds), *The Media in Britain*, Macmillan: Houndmills, 1999, pp201-207.

Ponting, C., *Secrecy in Britain*, Blackwell: Oxford, 1990.

Parekh, B., 'The Rushdie Affair: Research Agenda for Political Philosophy', *Political Studies*, Volume XXXVII, 1990, pp695-709.

Parekh, B., 'The Rushdie Affair and the British Press: Some Salutary Lessons', in B. Parekh (ed), *Free Speech*, Commission for Racial Equality: London, 1990, pp59-78.

Petley, J., 'The Regulation of Media Content', in J. Stokes and A. Reading (eds), *The Media in Britain*, Macmillan: Houndmills, 1999, pp143-157.

Rex, J., *Race and Ethnicity*, Open University Press: Milton Keynes, 1986.

Richards, D., 'Free Speech as Toleration', in W.J. Wuluchow (ed), *Free Expression: Essays on Law and Philosophy*, Oxford University Press: Oxford, 1994, pp31-57.

Robertson, D., *Dictionary of Politics*, Penguin: Harmondsworth, 1993.

Rowbotham, *The Past is Before Us*, Pandora: London, 1989.

Schwarzmantel, J., *The State in Contemporary Society*, Harvester: Hemel Hempstead, 1994.

Seaton, J., 'Broadcasting History', in J. Curran and J. Seaton, *Power without Responsibility*, Routledge: London, 1997, pp106-236.

Seldon, A., 'Northern Ireland' in B. Jones et al, *Politics UK*, Philip Allan: Hemel Hempstead, 1991, pp550-565.

Sheridan, G., 'CARM, race and the media: The story so far', in P. Cohen and C. Gardner (eds), *It aint half racist mum*, Comedia: London, 1982, pp1-4.

Sheridan, G., and Gardner, C., 'Press Freedom: A Socialist Strategy', in C. Gardner (ed), *Media, Politics and Culture*, Macmillan: London, 1979.

171

Smith, A., 'Censorship and the Great War', in P. Hyland and H. Sammells (eds), *Writing and Censorship in Britain*, Routledge: London, 1992, pp185-199.

Snoddy, R., *The Good, the Bad and the Unacceptable*, Faber and Faber: London, 1992 (1993 edition).

Solomos, J., and Back, L., *Racism and Society*, Macmillan: London, 1996.

Stevens, I.N., and Yardley, D.C.M., *The Protection of Liberty*, Blackwell: Oxford, 1982.

Statford, T., 'Women and the Press', in A. Belsey and R. Chadwick (eds), *Ethical Issues in Journalism and the Media*, Routledge: London, 1992, pp130-136.

Thackara, J., 'The Mass Media and Racism', in C. Gardner (ed), *Media, Politics and Culture*, Macmillan: London, 1979, pp108-118.

Troyna, B., 'Reporting Racism: The British way of life observed', in C. Husband (ed), *Race in Britain: Continuity and Change*, Hutchinson Education: London, 1987, pp275-291.

Tuchman, G., 'Women's depiction by the mass media', in H. Baehr and A. Gray (eds), *Turning it on*, Arnold: London, 1996, pp11-15.

Watson, J., *Media Communication*, Macmillan: Houndmills, 1998.

Webster, R., *A Brief History of Blasphemy*, Orwell Press: Suffolk, 1990.

Welsh, T., and Greenwood, W., *McNae's Essential Law for Journalists*, Butterworths, 1995 (13th edition).

Westin, A.F., *Privacy and Freedom*, Bodley Head: London, 1967.

White, A., 'Race, press freedom and the right of reply', in P. Cohen and C. Gardner (eds), *It aint half racist mum*, Comedia: London, 1982, pp80-83.

Whitehead, P., *The Writing on the Wall*, Michael Joseph: London, 1985.

Williams, G., *Political Theory in Retrospect*, Edward Elgar: Aldershot, 1991.

Williams, K., 'Something more important than truth', in A. Belsey and R. Chadwick (eds), *Ethical Issues in Journalism and the Media*, Routledge: London, 1992, pp154-170.

Williams, K., `The Light at the End of the Tunnel: The Mass Media, Public Opinion and the Vietnam War', in J. Eldridge (ed), *Getting the Message*, Routledge: London, London, 1993, pp305-328.

Williams, K., *Get me a murder a day !*, Arnold: London, 1998, pp138-140.

Newspaper and periodical articles

Alford, D., `Would you care if I had a beard ?', *Guardian*, 31.05.1999.

Anon, `Journalism and Patriotism', *Independent*, 18.01.1991 reprinted in B. Macarthur (ed), *Despatches from the Gulf War*, Bloomsbury: London, 1991, pp114-115.

Anon, `Liberalism can cope with skinheads', *Independent*, 16.04.1994.

Ahmed, K., `Sun to spend £2.5 m. to woo back readers', *Guardian*, 28.02.1998.

Cathcart, B., `Real Britannia: It starts with name calling. Where does it end ?', *Independent*, 23.07.1998.

Duncan, A., `If more reporters showed emotion, TV news wouldn't be losing so many viewers', *Radio Times*, 25.09.1998, pp8-12.

Forgan, L., `Trampling over Freedom', *Index on Censorship*, Volume 19, June/July 1990.

Fraser, D., `Power Players', *Guardian*, 8.02.1999.

Glaberson, W, `Fairness, bias and judgement: Grappling with the knotty issue of objectivity in journalism', *New York Times*, 12.12.1994

Harris, R., `Don't Shoot the Messenger', in B. Macarthur (ed), *Despatches from the Gulf War*, Bloomsbury: London, 1991, pp141-142.

Hastings, M., `Saddam and the Media', reprinted in B. Macarthur (ed), *Despatches from the Gulf War*, Bloomsbury: London, 1991, pp109-110.

Jacques, M., `The New Democracy', *The Observer*, 8.12.1998.

Knightley, P., `Sanitising the News', reprinted in B. Macarthur (ed), *Despatches from the Gulf War*, Bloomsbury: London, 1991, pp314-317.

Mack, T., `Women: Did you Ms. me ?', *Guardian*, 30.03.1999.

Mansfield, M., and Kogbara, D., `Speech of Freedom', *The Guardian*, 19.04.1997.

Marr, A., `A duty to hear muttonheads', *Independent*, 14.04.1994.

Pilger, J., `The Myth Makers', reprinted in B. Macarthur (ed), *Despatches from the Gulf War*, Bloomsbury: London, 1991, pp33-37.

Rushdie, S., `In Good Faith', *Independent on Sunday*, 4.12.1990

Sawyers, P., `Screen: Don't mention the N word', *Guardian*, 20.03.1998.

Searls, H., `The Rights and Wrongs of Privacy', *LM*, October 1997, pp15-19.

University Case Studies

Cloonan, M., `The Press part 1', *Case Studies for Politics 10*, University of York.

Cloonan, M., `The Press part 2', *Case Studies for Politics 11*, University of York.

Cloonan, M., `The Press part 3', *Case Studies for Politics 12*, University of York.

Internet sources

Goodman, E., `Pacific Coast Center Political Briefing Breakfast number 3, 14 March 1996', http:www.freedomforum/oakland/break3elleng.html

PCC Code of Practice, http://www.pcc.org.uk/complain/newcode.htm

Broadcast material (Arranged according to date of broadcast)

Manufacturing Consent, channel 4, 17.05.1993.

The Information War, BBC2, 16.08.1994.

And Finally Part 1: The Metropolitan Line, channel 4, 21.03.1995.

Myths and Memories of World War 2, BBC2, July 1995.
TV Images, BBC2, 15.06.1996
Have they got news for you, BBC1, 30.09.1996
Race Portrayal, BBC2, 6.10.1996
You Decide, ITV, 5.08.1997
BBC News, BBC1, 31.08.1997.
Royals and Reptiles: Part 4, channel 4, 9.11.1997
Auntie: The Inside Story of the BBC, Part 1-1922-1945, BBC1, 28.10.1997
Auntie: The Inside Story of the BBC: Part 4, BBC1,18.11.1997.
News and the Democratic Agenda, BBC2, 13.03.1998
Open Saturday: Hype, Hysteria and Fluffy Business, BBC1, 29.08.1998.